T0110709

Cambridge Elements ≡

Elements in Publishing and Book Culture
edited by
Samantha Rayner
University College London

OLD BOOKS AND DIGITAL PUBLISHING: EIGHTEENTH-CENTURY COLLECTIONS ONLINE

Stephen H. Gregg

Bath Spa University

CAMBRIDGE
UNIVERSITY PRESS

CAMBRIDGE
UNIVERSITY PRESS

University Printing House, Cambridge CB2 8BS, United Kingdom

One Liberty Plaza, 20th Floor, New York, NY 10006, USA

477 Williamstown Road, Port Melbourne, VIC 3207, Australia

314–321, 3rd Floor, Plot 3, Splendor Forum, Jasola District Centre,
New Delhi – 110025, India

79 Anson Road, #06–04/06, Singapore 079906

Cambridge University Press is part of the University of Cambridge.

It furthers the University's mission by disseminating knowledge in the pursuit of
education, learning, and research at the highest international levels of excellence.

www.cambridge.org
Information on this title: www.cambridge.org/9781108720694
DOI: 10.1017/9781108767415

© Stephen H. Gregg 2020

This publication is in copyright. Subject to statutory exception
and to the provisions of relevant collective licensing agreements,
no reproduction of any part may take place without the written
permission of Cambridge University Press.

First published 2020

A catalogue record for this publication is available from the British Library.

ISBN 978-1-108-72069-4 Paperback
ISSN 2514-8524 (online)
ISSN 2514-8516 (print)

Cambridge University Press has no responsibility for the persistence or accuracy of
URLs for external or third-party internet websites referred to in this publication
and does not guarantee that any content on such websites is, or will remain,
accurate or appropriate.

Old Books and Digital Publishing: Eighteenth-Century Collections Online

Elements in Publishing and Book Culture

DOI: 10.1017/9781108767415

First published online: November 2020

Stephen H. Gregg

Bath Spa University

Author for correspondence: Stephen H. Gregg, s.gregg@bathspa.ac.uk

ABSTRACT: This is a history of Eighteenth Century Collections Online (ECCO), a database of more than 180,000 titles. Published by Gale in 2003, it has had an enormous impact on the study of the eighteenth century. Like many commercial digital archives, ECCO's continuing development obscures its precedents. This Element examines its prehistory as first a computer catalogue of eighteenth-century print, and then as a commercial microfilm collection, before moving to the digitisation and development of the interfaces to ECCO, as well as Gale's various partnerships and licensing deals. An essential aspect of this Element is how it explores the sociocultural and technological debates around access to old books from the 1930s to the present: Stephen Gregg demonstrates how these contexts powerfully shape the way ECCO works to this day. This Element's aim is to make us better users and readers of digital archives.

KEYWORDS: books, remediation, history, digital publishing, eighteenth century

© Stephen H. Gregg 2020

ISBNs: 9781108720694 (PB), 9781108767415 (OC)

ISSNs: 2514-8524 (online), 2514-8516 (print)

Contents

Timeline

1976	Proposal for an eighteenth-century short title catalogue. Cataloguing on the Eighteenth-Century Short Title Catalogue (18thC STC) begins in earnest from around 1978.
1981	British Library signs contract with Research Publications (RPI) to microfilm its eighteenth-century books based on the 18thC STC. Microfilming and production on the collection, called The Eighteenth Century, begins in 1982.
1987	18thC STC cataloguing expanded to include pre-1700 material.
1987–8	Microfilming operation expanded.
1994	The 18thC STC renamed the English Short Title Catalogue (ESTC).
1995	RPI becomes Primary Source Media (PSM).
1996	Thomson Learning decides to begin digitising its collections.
1998	PSM, Information Access Company, and Gale Research merge to form Gale Group, part of Thomson Learning.
1998	ProQuest launches Early English Books Online (EEBO).
1999	Text Creation Partnership (TCP) formed.
2000	ECCO digitisation begins.
2001–2	Gale Group becomes Thomson-Gale.
2003–4	Eighteenth Century Collections Online published.
2004–10	TCP schedule for transcribing and publishing ECCO-TCP texts.
2006–9	UK organisation Jisc purchases ECCO files under license.
2007	Thomson Group sells Thomson Learning to private equity firms and it is renamed Cengage Learning. Gale becomes an imprint of Cengage.
2007	Cross-search with EEBO added to interface.

2009	ECCO II publishes more than 46,000 extra titles from scans done between 2003 and 2009. Subject field added. Optical character recognition (OCR) software replaced. ESTC and ECCO metadata enhanced by adding Library of Congress subject headings.
2010	End of microfilming programme.
2010	BiblioLife produces print-on-demand copies of ECCO titles.
2010	18thConnect website launched.
2011	Jisc Historic Books platform launched.
2011	TCP releases *c.*2,200 ECCO-TCP texts.
2014	Jisc Historic Books redesigned and relaunched as Historical Texts.
2014	Gale launches 'Textual Data Analysis' hard drives.
2015	Gale offers an additional ECCO interface option called Artemis.
2016	Artemis renamed Gale Primary Sources.
2019	Gale Digital Scholar Lab (beta) platform launched.
2020	Gale begins digitising a further *c.*90,000 books for future publication as ECCO III.
2020	Original 'stand-alone' ECCO interface scheduled to be turned off.

1 Introduction

Eighteenth Century Collections Online (ECCO) is an online database published by Gale-Cengage. First published in 2003, it gives access via subscribing libraries to 184,536 titles of material printed between 1700 and 1800, comprising the text and digital images of their pages. In 2020 2,092 institutions and consortia in forty-two countries subscribe; in 2019 around 7.7 million search results, images, or texts were retrieved worldwide (De Mowbray, 2020a). It is arguably the largest single online collection of specifically eighteenth-century material available via academic institutions and has had a profound impact on how researchers conduct scholarship of the period. A history of a digital resource like ECCO is important because if we are at all interested in old books, and assuming we're also aware of the exponential increase in accessing old books via resources like ECCO, then we should be interested in why digitised books look the way they do and the difference that makes, how ECCO works the way it does, and what we can – and can't – do with these books.

Eighteenth Century Collections Online is deeply rooted in a longer history of representing eighteenth-century books, the effect of which can still be traced in the way ECCO works, since it is based upon a commercial microfilm collection, The Eighteenth Century, the contents of which were selected on the basis of a computerised cataloguing programme, the Eighteenth-Century Short Title Catalogue (18thC STC). As Sarah Werner and Matthew Kirschenbaum argue, we cannot 'posit a transcendental "digital" that somehow stands outside the historical and material legacies of other artifacts and phenomena'; rather, the digital is a *'frankly messy complex of extensions and extrusions of prior media and technologies'* (Kirschenbaum & Werner, 2014: 408; my emphasis).

This is why this book starts with a 'prehistory' in order to understand the twentieth-century contexts of earlier media technologies, the changing cultures of scholarship, and what was driving commercial academic publishing. The first section draws out two significant factors from the 18thC STC (begun in 1976). The first is that decisions had to be made about what material it would include and what material it would not – these decisions would subsequently affect the scope and nature of ECCO's content.

The second is that the catalogue was from the outset a digital project, but that presented a challenge: how would the idiosyncratic features of books produced by the hand press translate into standardised machine-readable data? This metadata (data *about* something, rather than the thing itself) would eventually shape how ECCO could be searched as well as how users apprehend the nature of old books when they are digital images. The second section moves to Research Publication's (RPI) microfilm collection, The Eighteenth Century (published from 1982 onwards). It sets out the scholarly and commercial contexts for the development of this new media technology from the 1930s to the end of the twentieth century, illuminating the arguments of scholars, libraries, and microfilm companies for how this new technology would enable the preservation of and enable a wider access to research materials and old books.

At this point it's worth establishing why a focus on the books within ECCO is important. My approach to the *idea* of the book is predicated on a series of axioms:

1. The form of the printed book is a particular medium for the words within (as opposed to, say, a scroll or an audiobook).
2. The meaning of a book does not solely consist of the words within; the material form and the design of the book itself have meaning.
3. Transform the book into another medium ('remediation') and you change the meanings of the book.

It's for these reasons that this book, in the chapter 'Bookishness', looks at some case studies of individual eighteenth-century books in order to exemplify the effects of the 18thC STC and the microfilming programme on how users apprehend the physicality – the material life – of hand-press books as they are presented as digital images in ECCO. Part of this is a study of how users navigate between the image of a book and its record (spoiler: there is no seamless 'fit'), but it also emphasises the effect of human agency and human decisions about technology on how old books look in ECCO. In this sense my conceptual framework for this history is indebted to the powerful arguments for the critical potential of book history D. F. McKenzie made in his lectures of 1985, in which he proposed that bibliography should concern itself with a 'sociology of texts'. I start with his point that the term 'texts' should go beyond the printed text to encompass the very broadest set of human communication media and even – most vital for us – 'computer-stored information'; there is, he argues, 'no evading the challenge which those new forms have created' (McKenzie, 1999: 13). The discipline of bibliography 'studies texts as recorded forms, and the processes of their transmission, including their production and reception' (12). Perhaps the strongest argument for my history is that a 'sociology of texts' should allow 'us to describe not only the technical but the social processes of their transmission', and it 'directs us to consider the human motives and interactions which texts involve at every stage of their production, transmission, and consumption. It alerts us to the role of institutions, and their own complex structures, in affecting the forms of social discourse, past and present' (McKenzie, 1999: 13, 15). Sociocultural forces, institutions, technology, and human agency all play their part in this history.

Eighteenth Century Collections Online – or any digital entity – is not a static or an unchanging entity: it *has* a history. The rapidity with which commercial publishing technology supersedes older versions of itself has meant that some circumstances of its development are now obscure and others are irrecoverable. Tellingly, a part of ECCO will become invisible from 2020 when its original interface is scheduled to be turned off: it will *literally* be history. So this book is partly an act of recovery. The third chapter, 'Beginnings', turns to the development of ECCO itself. In the first section, I examine the immediate contexts that shaped how ECCO was to work and to be sold. It was decisively influenced by the downward movement of the academic publishing market and the emerging so-called disruptive technologies in the 1990s (Bower & Christensen, 1995). I focus on the techno-commercial choices facing Gale by illustrating contemporary digital resources created by two of its key commercial competitors in academic publishing of the time: Chadwyck-Healey and ProQuest. In addition, some aspects of how ECCO works 'under the hood' are – in common with many digital products – simply invisible to the public. The chapter goes on to explain Gale's digitisation of the microfilm collection, discussing the problems created by the use of optical character recognition (OCR) software to automatically create text from digital images of old books, how its metadata was structured, and how ECCO's original search interface worked.

The chapter 'Interfacing' takes us forward to Gale's development of ECCO after 2010, but also returns us to the issues of access. First, it focuses on the conglomerate of deals and collaborations between Gale and various partners, all of which broadly attempted to address concerns about *who* could access ECCO, as well as *how* ECCO might be used and interrogated, including the Text Creation Partnership, Jisc, and the print--on-demand deal with BiblioLife. This chapter's last section discusses the effects and meanings of the rise of the platform: this enabled the cross-searching of aggregated digital resources in a single package, but also a new way of interfacing with data and texts that was – for Gale's platforms – influenced by their belated engagement with the scholarly field of digital humanities. However, the platform produces a crucial tension between two ways of understanding and using old books: the bibliographical (or the 'bookishness' of books) and the textual. I finish by considering the politics of how these platforms represent early print history, drawing on the insights of postcolonial digital humanities, and reminding us that the Anglocentric nature of digital resources like ECCO is a product – a partially obscured one – of human decisions made in its antecedents, the 18thC STC and the microfilm collection. Indeed, throughout the book I've tried to avoid the suggestion that technological change is the only driving force in the twentieth and twenty-first centuries; instead I hope to have demonstrated that in ECCO's history – indeed, in the history of remediating and publishing old books – technology is inextricable from culture and human decisions.

I intend my history of a digital resource to mirror the methodology of bibliography. As W. W. Greg argued:

> the object of bibliographical study is, I believe, to recon-struct for each particular book the history of its life, to make it reveal in its most intimate detail the story of its birth and adventures as the material vehicle of the living word. (Greg, 1945: 27)

Like the life history of old books, I hope to reveal the intimate details of the life history of ECCO: this book is partly an argument for the application of bibliography to digital entities, conceived as a 'material vehicle of the living word'.[1] Looking over my introduction I hope it's also clear that the status of entities like ECCO and their digitised books actually challenges the notion of a linear, progressive history. First, as Bonnie Mak has noted of books that have been subject to remediation, past and present versions of the same book copy exist simultaneously; in our case, as catalogue, as record, as microfilm, as digital images, as digital text, and even as a print-on-demand copy (Mak, 2014: 1516, 1519). This is echoed in the movement between past and present when we discuss ECCO's place within wider historical contexts. Alan Liu's comment about how we imagine and write narratives of media is suggestive: 'the best stories of new media encounter – emergent *from messy, reversible entanglements* with history, socio-politics, and subjectivity – do not go from beginning to end, and so are not really stories at all' (Liu, 2013: 16, my emphasis).

My aim is to speak to people interested in old books, people interested in how digitised collections of books work, and people interested in the history of how new media technologies have affected academic publishing. With such a broad reader in mind, I have tried not to assume any expert knowledge of old books, technology, or academic publishing even though this means taking the odd digression to explain a microhistory of file formats, or microfilm publishing, or some bibliographical terminology. The challenge of my history is to trace the digressive reverberation of ideas and debates that surrounded how we access and what we do with old books, and the chronological messiness of books whose lives have been subject to constant change. But this history is more than that; it is also an argument that we should better grasp the nature of something students and scholars rely upon for their understanding of eighteenth-century print and an argument for recovering, reading, and researching digital resources critically.

[1] This book's methodology is indebted to the interface between book history and digital humanities; in addition to those cited here see, for example, the work by Ryan Cordell, Johanna Drucker, Alan Galey, Jerome McGann, and Whitney Trettien.

2 Prehistory

Cataloguing the Eighteenth Century

Eighteenth Century Collections Online is based on a microfilm collection produced between 1982 and the early 2000s. This film collection itself was based on a catalogue of books begun in 1976 called the Eighteenth-Century Short Title Catalogue, under the editorship of Robin Alston, consultant at the British Library, co-edited with Henry Snyder in the United States. From 1987 this project expanded to include material printed before 1700 and was eventually renamed the English Short Title Catalogue (ESTC). In its current form the ESTC is an online catalogue of printed material published from the fifteenth century to the end of the eighteenth century. It's difficult to capture the sheer scale of the ESTC and its ambition: looking back over the project from 2003, Thomas Tanselle reaches for numbers: the 'file (achieved at a cost of about 30 million dollars) consists of some 435,000 records, indicating the location of over 2,000,000 copies in 1,600 libraries around the world' (in Snyder & Smith, 2003: xi). Currently it comprises more than 480,000 records from 2,000 libraries worldwide.[2] However, the project was initially confined to material printed between 1700 and 1800, and because it is this that shaped the underlying nature of ECCO, this history concentrates on the catalogue project before 1987.[3]

The first discussions about the possibility of a catalogue that would cover the eighteenth century began as early as 1962 amongst members of the Bibliographical Society, and such a catalogue was perceived as the logical next step from the two Short Title Catalogues (STCs) covering material printed between 1475 and 1640 (Pollard and Redgrave) and 1641 and 1700 (Wing). However, it was from 1975 that the catalogue got the necessary backing to start. More significantly, the discussions and plans by the leading editors for the 18thC STC emphasised the necessity that it be produced as

---

[2] British Library – Projects – English Short Title Catalogue: www.bl.uk/projects/ english-short-title-catalogue?_ga=2.29691066.42946434.1568626674– 1896136714.1415013819 [accessed 27 May 2020].

[3] I refer to the project between 1976 and 1987 as the 18thC STC, and the project as it currently exists as the ESTC.

an electronic file so that it could be managed and queried by computers (Alston & Janetta, 1978; Crump, 2003: 54; Snyder, 2003: 21–30; Alston, 2004). One of the most significant aspects of the 18thC STC is that it was deeply influenced by developments in computer-aided library cataloguing and online networked computer systems in the 1960s. The technology of machine-readable catalogue records would be an essential aspect of how metadata (that is, information *about* an object, distinct from the object itself) works alongside images and text of old books in digital archives and collections of the twenty-first century.

Korshin's 1976 grant application to get the 18thC STC off the ground included the participation of Hank Epstein, the director of the Stanford University computing team (Alston, 2004). Notably, the Stanford Research Institute was the first, in 1963, to demonstrate an 'online bibliographical search system', an 'online full-text search system', and systems that could be used remotely over long distances, and it was the first to use a screen display for interaction between human and computer (Bourne & Hahn, 2003: 14–15). In 1978 the Stanford-based Research Libraries Group developed an online networked database called the Research Libraries Information Network (RLIN).[4] In 1980 the 18thC STC at the British Library formed an important collaboration with the group, and by 1985 US and UK teams of the 18thC STC were able to edit the same file interactively online (Crump, 2003: 55).

Technological solutions to managing information had been the subject of both visionary projects and practical application since the end of the nineteenth century; two particular figures are often cited as seminal thinkers in this field. One is Paul Otlet (1868–1944) who, with Henri La Fontaine, designed a huge card catalogue in the 1890s entitled the 'Universal Bibliographic Repertory'. Otlet worked with Robert Goldschmidt on microfilming in the 1920s and 1930s, after which Otlet published a collection of his essays on the future of information science, *Traité de Documentation*, in 1934. The other is Vannevar Bush (1890–1974): in 1945 he proposed – but never built – a machine called 'Memex' that would

---

[4] 'Online' before the birth of the Internet and the Web merely means that two or more computers were directly connected via a closed network.

display microfilm and that also had the capability to apply, search, and retrieve keywords about the information on the microfilms (Deegan & Sutherland, 2009: 125–6; Borsuk, 2018: 209–13).

However, more significant than either of these men for the future of library information was Henriette Avram (1919–2006). Her career as one of the first computer programmers led eventually to designing library information systems at the Library of Congress in 1965. It was here that she developed the first – and what would become the standard – computerised library cataloguing system throughout the world: MAchine Readable Catalogue (MARC) (Rather & Wiggins, 1989). Before the advent of computer-aided catalogues libraries used card catalogues; the details about a book, for instance, would be recorded on a three-by-five card. The system for ensuring all libraries had access to and could update library catalogue records involved card-copying services and transporting duplicate card records by mail. By contrast a record that a machine can read can be disseminated and centralised much more easily. A MARC record is divided up into coded fields each of which contains a designated type of information, such as author, title, library location, subject, and many more. Avram's pioneering work necessitated a thorough understanding of computing *and* the principles of bibliographical cataloguing. The MAchine Readable Catalogue, then, was not only about designing a record to be parsed by a computer; it also set the standard for bibliographical records that libraries across the world would follow. The eventual result is the kind of human-readable record you can see on the online ESTC catalogue entry for the 1789 issue of Patrick Browne's *The Civil and Natural History of Jamaica* (Figure 1). Later I use this book to explore the relationship between the physical book and its record.

In fact, Alston discussed the 18thC STC with Henriette Avram in 1977 (Alston, 2004). In the earliest discussions the catalogue was to adopt the principles of the seminal catalogue of early print: Pollard and Redgrave's 1926 *A Short-Title Catalogue of Books Printed in England, Scotland, & Ireland and of English Books Printed Abroad, 1475–1640*. But it was clear that the 18thC STC would be a computerised catalogue and that therefore records would follow the much more detailed standards required by MARC (Alston & Janetta, 1978: 24–6). In his 1981 lecture 'Computers and Bibliography' Alston was adamant that computing would enable more

ESTC System No.	006359980
ESTC Citation No.	T89758
Author - personal	*Browne, Patrick, 1720?-1790.
Title	*The civil and natural history of Jamaica. Containing I. An accurate description of that island, its situation, and soil; with a brief account of its former and present state, government, revenues, produce, and trade. II. An history of the natural productions, including the various sorts of native fossils; perfect and imperfect vegetables; quadrupeds, birds, fishes, reptiles, and insects; with their properties and uses in mechanics, diet, and physic. By Patrick Browne, M.D. illustrated with forty-nine copper plates; in which the most curious productions are represented of their natural sizes, delineated immediately from the objects, by George Dionysius Ehret. There are now added complete Linnaean indexes, and a large and accurate map of the island.
Publisher/year	*London : sold by B. White and Son, at Horace's Head, Fleet-Street, M.DCC,LXXXIX. [1789]
Physical descr.	[6],viii,503,[47]p.,plates ; map ; 2°.
General note	With a half-title and four additional indexes.
	With a list of subscribers.
	A reissue of the sheets of the 1756 edition, with a new titlepage.
	Part of the 1756 edition was printed by William Bowyer; his records show 738 copies printed on crown and 12 on demy; John Hart may also have printed part of the edition.
Citation/references	Goldsmiths', 13843
	Maslen and Lancaster. Bowyer ledgers, 4023
Surrogates	Microfilm. Woodbridge, Conn. : Primary Source Microfilm, an imprint of Gale Group, 2002. 1 reel ; 35 mm. Unit 361. (The Eighteenth Century ; reel 12612 , no. 02).
	Microfilm. New Haven, CT Research Publications, Inc., 1976. 1 reel ; 35mm. (Goldsmiths'-Kress Library of Economic Literature ; reel 1412, no. 13843).
Subject	*Tropical medicine -- Early works to 1800.
	*Medical climatology -- Early works to 1800.
	*Natural history -- Jamaica -- Early works to 1800.
Copies - Brit.Isles	*Brighton Central Library
	*British Library
	*Cambridge University Library (includes Sir Geoffrey Keynes Collection, British & Foreign Bible Society, & Peterborough Cathedral)
	*Glasgow University Library
	*National Library of Ireland
	*National Library of Scotland

Figure 1 ESTC record, Patrick Browne, *The Civil and Natural History of Jamaica*, 1789 (screenshot, 22 May 2020)

powerful scholarship. Alongside the inventions of writing and printing as technologies of knowledge, Alston noted, 'we have now added a third (and by comparison with the former two) quite remarkable one: the storage, and virtually instant retrieval, of information about the present and the past in electro-mechanical form, and the mechanical aids available to assist in this process are now formidable – more powerful than anything we have known' (Alston, 1981a: 379).

Using machine-readable records meant that users could perform much more sophisticated searches than were possible with card catalogues (Zeeman, 1980: 4). In addition, cataloguers, 'keen to facilitate greater access to the online records, tended subconsciously (perhaps) to transcribe long titles', enabling users to conduct complex keyword searches (Crump, 1988: 5).

However, using MARC for the 18thC STC would not be a seamless fit. It's worth reminding ourselves that each book in this period was handmade, the product of a series of processes which depended 'upon a complex sequence of events, all of which were determined by humans capable of fallibility, stupidity, laziness, inconsistency, disobedience' (Alston, 1981a: 372). These included the making of paper, ink, and metal type, as well as composing type into sentences, locking those sentences into a frame, using the press to make each sheet, proofreading, and compiling it all into a book (Figures 2 & 3).

Figure 2 Metal type

Figure 3 Hand press, *c.*1700s

As Alston notes, 'data must be stored within a system hospitable to eccentric evidence' (Alston, 1981a: 379). Books of the hand-press period and their records are 'eccentric' in the sense of being 'Irregular, anomalous' (OED, 6a). That is to say that – leaving aside editions and variants – the potential disparity between copies of the same book requires a method of cataloguing that can register such nonconformity. Alston emphasised the human agency involved in making books in order to highlight the limitations of the new 'bibliographical networks' that require 'rigid' cataloguing standards (Alston, 1981a: 373). The implicit tension, then, was between information scientists for whom an isolated record sufficed to stand in for all copies and variations of a handmade book, and scholars for whom this would be a meaningless abstraction rather than a record of a book's material life history – the purpose of bibliography that W. W. Greg persuasively defined (Greg, 1945: 27). As Alston and Janetta put it in their outline of the 18thC STC, 'the larger purpose, in which that record can reveal contextually its ancestry and its offspring, is for most students of cultural history of far greater significance' (1978: 29).

The sheer scale of the print output of the period meant that the 18thC STC had to delimit its scope in a variety of ways. Alston and Jannetta noted that the 18thC STC aimed to 'describe a corpus of printing more than ten times the size' of the two existing STCs of pre-1700 material (Alston & Janetta, 1978: 24). It set generic limits to the material and would not include: engraved material; printed forms, such as licences, warrants, certificates, etc.; trade and visiting cards, tickets, invitations, currency (although advertisements were to be included); playbills and concert programmes; playing cards, games, and puzzles (Alston & Janetta, 1978: 16–17). More significantly, it constructed its scope along geographic and linguistic lines. It would include:

1. All relevant items printed in the British Isles in any language;
2. All relevant items printed in Colonial America, the United States (1776–1800), and Canada in any language;
3. All relevant items printed in territories governed by Britain during any period of the eighteenth century in any language;
4. All relevant items printed wholly or partly in English, or other British vernaculars, in any part of the world.

Its Anglo-American foundation is clear here, as well as an unconscious legacy of British colonialism in the continuing idea of the British Commonwealth. For Alston the catalogue was also tied to the function of a new British national library. Conscious that the project came on the heels of the British Library's creation after it was separated from the British Museum in 1973, he felt it was the new institution's 'responsibility for the production of the national bibliographic record' (quoted in Crump, in

Snyder, 2003: 49). Indeed, cataloguing is not a neutral process. Molly Hardy's reflection on the cataloguing and marginalisation of African-American printers usefully highlights how 'our organization of data, no matter how neutral we imagine it to be, is built out of and therefore reflects on a particular moment' and is therefore organised 'within a system that can never itself be neutral because its creation, like the data it captures, is a humanist endeavor' (Hardy, 2016).

The 18thC STC project was a bold attempt to catalogue in as much detail as possible the 'ancestry and . . . offspring' of thousands of printed works. But it is worth emphasising that a catalogue record is a representation of a book, and the catalogue as a whole was a select representation of the printed output of the period. Moreover, the way in which the electronic bibliographic data of the 18thC STC was able to capture the 'eccentric evidence' of hand-press books would directly shape how readers apprehended the nature of the books when they were transformed into microfilm images and, subsequently, into digital images and metadata in ECCO. In addition, the careful delineation of the scope of the 18thC STC would directly shape the content of both the microfilm collection and ECCO.

Books into Images: Microfilming in the Twentieth Century

In 1981 it was announced that the British Library Board had approved the bid from Research Publications (RPI) to 'reproduce in microform a comprehensive library of eighteenth-century texts based on ESTC'. Robin Alston, the UK editor of the 18thC STC, was, initially at least, the director of the project.[5] Alston envisioned that the 18thC STC online catalogue would be a gateway to the filmed copy: 'users – whether libraries or scholars – will be given a unique opportunity to acquire access to both bibliographical records and whole-text reproduction' (Alston, 1981b: 2). Alston also hoped that microfilm would preserve the fragile, rare books at the British Library from 'the unequal struggle between book and reader', anticipating that 'the proposed microform library will have a tremendous impact on the total conservation effort' (Alston, 1981b: 3). Alston's announcement emphasised access and preservation. His vision for the microfilming of the 18thC STC echoed the

---

[5] Alston was with the project only one year (Alston, 2004: n. 121).

technological progressivism of a number of scholars, librarians, and publishers who promoted microfilm as the pre-eminent solution to the preservation of and access to rare books in the twentieth century.

Cultural demands of fidelity and accessibility have driven changes in the technology of reproduction since the 1700s and consequently have raised questions about how old books are represented as visual images (McKitterick, 2013). Key to these issues was the application of photography to creating facsimiles. As David McKitterick argues, by the late 1800s the lure of the image had a profound effect: by 'seeming to withdraw one of the veils between original and reproduction, replacing human intervention by chemical and mechanical processes, photography offered a new kind of reliability, and even a new kind of truth' (McKitterick, 2013: 127). The promise of absolute fidelity as a kind of preservation of or even substitute for the original, combined with cheapness and therefore accessibility, would not only spur the production and dissemination of photographic facsimiles of old books in the nineteenth century, but formed the driving arguments of both the twentieth-century microfilming and digitisation projects too.

What led microfilm to be the dominant reproduction technology of the twentieth century? It had been the subject of interest since the invention of photography, although early experiments were perceived as novelties. But it was the confluence of technology and sociocultural forces in 1920s and 1930s America that provided the conditions for the beginnings of the micropublishing industry.[6] One of the most significant moments for this history is the meeting in 1934 between historian Robert C. Binkley, secretary of the Joint Committee on Materials for Research (JCMR), and Eugene B. Power, of Edwards Brothers publishing: it was at this meeting that various developments in microfilming were brought together, and it was arguably the catalyst of a new publishing industry.[7] They discussed the microfilming experiments by R. H. Draeger of

---

[6] In 1935 a deputy keeper at the British Museum 'expressed regret at the fact that the British Museum was lagging behind in this field' (Harris, 1998: 530–1).

[7] They had first met during the 1931 JCMR conference: present were scholars, librarians, printers, and publishers. Out of this came Binkley's report *Methods of Reproducing Research Materials*, published by Edward Brothers in 1931. This was a comprehensive survey of the most up-to-date reproduction technologies,

the US Navy, and the Recordak Corporation's 'Check-O-Graph' machine that photographed cheques on a continuous 16 mm film, which enabled banks for the first time to verify cheques and to counter fraud (Power, 1990: 23–6). They also discussed the 'Bibliofilm Service' established by the librarian Claribel Barnett to copy the records of the hearings of the National Recovery and the Agricultural Adjustment Administrations (Binkley, 1936: 134). Binkley described its operation in this manner: 'a page of print or typescript is photographically reduced twenty-three diameters in size, being copies on a strip of film ½ inch wide and one or two hundred feet long. The micro-copies are rendered legible by projection. A machine throws an enlarged image downward on a table, where the reader finds it just as legible as the original page' (Binkley, 1935/1948: 183) (Figure 4).

Hearing about these projects in late 1934 provided Power with his notion of a radical new way of publishing:

Figure 4 Microfilming public records, New Jersey, 1937

including microfilm, and it included a detailed discussion of costs, note-taking and legibility, and the pros and cons of various projection technologies and storage methods.

If the film in [the] projector were a positive instead of a negative,
it would be projected onto the screen black-on-white, reading
exactly like the page of a book. I could photograph a page and
print a positive-film copy for the customer, keeping the negative
in my file to be duplicated over and over again in filling future
requests. There would be no need, as there was in traditional
publishing, to maintain a warehouse inventory of finished copies
or to rephotograph the original material. Each copy made would
be to fill a specific order. I could keep a vault full of negatives;
therefore, no title need ever go out of print. (Power, 1990: 27,
emphasis in original)

Power had already been photographing old books as early as 1931, but
systems like Draeger's or Recordak's could do this on a bigger scale: the
technology of bulk photography, the mass storage of filmed documents, and
the ability to print the document – or book – when required would 'make
possible the production of a single, readable book at a low unit cost' (Power,
1990: 17). It sounds uncannily like digital print-on-demand books of the early
twenty-first century available via Amazon. Power began his own microfilm
project based on the books catalogued by Pollard and Redgrave's STC and
started operations at the British Museum in 1935. After a number of US
libraries took up a subscription service for these films, in 1938 Power left
Edwards Brothers and formed University Microfilms Incorporated (UMI),
arguably the most successful international microfilm publisher of scholarly
materials (Power, 1990: 28–9, 32–5). It is perhaps significant for the history of
academic publishing that the large-scale reproduction of old books was
undertaken by a commercial business. As we will see in the chapter called
'Interfacing', the effect of commercial proprietorship over scholarly materials
becomes a significant issue in relation to digitisation projects.

The dream that technology could offer more universal access to knowledge was perhaps most stirringly articulated by H. G. Wells in his 1937
essay 'The Idea of a Permanent World Encyclopedia':

There is no practical obstacle whatever now to the creation
of an efficient index to *all* human knowledge, ideas and

achievements, to the creation, that is, of a complete planetary memory for all mankind. And not simply an index; the direct reproduction of the thing itself can be summoned to any properly prepared spot. A microfilm ... can be duplicated from the records and sent anywhere, and thrown enlarged upon the screen so that the student may study it in every detail. (Wells, 1938: 86)

However, Binkley's 1935 paper 'New Tools for Men of Letters' (based on an earlier memorandum of 1934) is even more prescient. It is perhaps the earliest and fullest published reflection on access, scholarship, and new media technology. For both Power and Binkley the challenge was to figure out how to reproduce and distribute low-demand works and difficult-to-access scholarly materials:

[T]he Western scholar's problem is not to get hold of the books that everyone else has read or is reading but rather to procure materials that hardly anyone else would think of looking at ... Printing technique, scholarly activities, and library funds have increased the amount of available material at a tremendous rate, but widening interests and the three centuries' accumulation of out-of-print titles have increased the number of desired but inaccessible books at an even greater rate. (Binkley, 1935/1948: 182)

While 'New Tools' considers a variety of reproduction technologies, microfilm is proposed as the best solution because it 'offers the reader a book production system more elastic than anything he has had since the fifteenth century; it will respond to the demand for a unique copy, regardless of other market prospects. So the scholar in a small town can have resources of great metropolitan libraries at his disposal' (Binkley, 1935/1948: 184).

This last remark about the 'small town' scholar is uniquely Binkley's. His aim in harnessing the new technology of microfilm is to extend access: 'Let there be included among our objectives', he argues, 'not only a bathroom in every home and a car in every garage but a scholar in every schoolhouse and a man of letters in every town. Towards this end technology offers new devices and points the way' (Binkley, 1935/1948: 197).

In addition to access, issues of conservation and preservation drove the tremendous expansion of microfilming throughout the twentieth century, such as preserving the rare materials endangered by the wars in Europe (Power, 1990: 117, 125–7), preserving newspapers at the British Museum from the late 1940s (Harris, 1998: 601–2), and, indeed, conserving the books in the British Library catalogued by the 18thC STC (Alston, 1981b: 3). In 1988 Patricia M. Battin argued to a US committee that the fragility of books means that 'it is the record of our shared symbolic code itself that is decaying and endangered. We cannot expect the societal cohesiveness that comes from a symbolic code if the record that comprises it is lost to us' (Battin, 1988). Technology, it is implied, can save the texts of Western culture. In 2001 there was a burst of public debate about the effects of a mass microfilming project, spurred by Nicholson Baker's provocative attack on libraries' disposal of books and newspapers. Baker's aim was to expose the ostensible fragility and brittleness of books and newspapers as a myth and to reveal the libraries' microfilming (and digitisation) programmes as a kind of technological zealotry (Baker, 2001).[8]

But what was being preserved: the information (the ideas and words) or the material medium (books, documents)? In this light, Robert Binkley's conception of the scholar's attitude to the nature of their material is striking. 'All the documents' which the scholar uses, he states,

> are for him 'materials for research,' He does not care whether they are printed or typewritten or in manuscript form, whether durable or perishable, whether original or photostat, so long as they are legible. Whether the edition is large or small, whether the library buys, begs, or borrows the material makes no difference to him so long as he can have it in hand when he wants it. (Binkley, 1936: 1)

---

[8] There was subsequent heated debate in the *Times Literary Supplement* on similar projects in Britain (Deegan & Sutherland, 2009: 49–50).

In this conception the medium of reproduction does not affect the content or meaning of the document. The physical nature of the document or book is of little importance: access is everything. At the same time as this rush to microfilm, others were alarmed by what might be lost by the new media technologies of reproduction (Gitelman, 2014: 63–4). A technology that can reproduce ad infinitum identical images of the original object in the name of accessibility poses questions about the relationship between original and copy. This is the burden of Walter Benjamin's 1936 essay 'The Work of Art in the Age of Mechanical Reproduction'. The essay is largely a response to the increasing popularity of film, but it argues that photography has precipitated 'the most profound change' on the authenticity of the work of art. This, he says

> is the essence of all that is transmissible from its beginning, ranging from its substantive duration to its testimony to the history which it has experienced. Since the historical testimony rests on the authenticity, the former, too, is jeopardized by reproduction when substantive duration ceases to matter ... that which withers in the age of mechanical reproduction is the aura of the work of art. This is a symptomatic process whose significance points beyond the realm of art. One might generalize by saying: the technique of reproduction detaches the reproduced object from the domain of tradition. By making many reproductions it substitutes a plurality of copies for a unique existence. (Benjamin, 1970: 221, 223)

For scholars of the book the processes of reproduction potentially pose a similar danger to the 'historical testimony' of the 'unique' object of the book. In 1941 – at the same time UMI was busily filming at the British Museum – bibliographer William A. Jackson had been asked to comment on the technology of microfilm which had been 'contagiously expounded.' He enumerated the failures of two-dimensional black-and-white film shot in one plane to capture variations in the tone, colour, or quality of paper, to prevent the introduction of stray marks and blots, and finally, to reproduce the 'intangible' features of a book perceptible only by touch (Jackson, 1941: 281, 285). In his 2001 article 'Not the Real Thing' Thomas G. Tanselle cited the example of the American preservation project under Battin, pointing out that this project of microfilming 'was not designed to save books but rather the texts in them'. Tanselle argued that such projects suffer from a 'confusion surrounding the relation between books (physical objects) and verbal works (texts made of language)' and suggested a 'pernicious' perception 'that a text can be transferred without loss from one object . . . to another' (Tanselle, 2001).

We've come to a striking set of parallel worlds: on one hand the scholar-technologists like Power and Binkley, and on the other theorists like Benjamin and scholar-bibliographers like Jackson and Tanselle. Binkley and Power clearly had in mind a method of disseminating costly or hard-to-access scholarly documents. Their aim was not essentially bibliographic – the concerns of historians of the book like Jackson and Tanselle – but 'informatic' (Gitelman, 2014: 63). One question this book pursues is this: how would surrogates such as filmed books be used? As Deegan and Sutherland put it, 'Under what circumstances or what purposes is a facsimile a satisfactory surrogate for the object itself? . . . Are we preserving features of the objects themselves or only the information they contain?' (Deegan & Sutherland, 2009: 157–8).

The Eighteenth Century: Microfilming the Catalogue

Research Publications was awarded the British Library contract for filming the 18thC STC. Robin Alston had been responsible for assessing bids for the filming in late 1980 from Chadwyck-Healey Ltd., University Microfilms International (UMI), Newspaper Archive Developments Ltd., and RPI (Alston, 2004: n. 119, 120, 121).[9] Samuel Freedman founded RPI in 1966, in Meckler's words, 'for the express purpose of micropublishing significant archives and documents'. Significantly for Alston's decision, RPI's series Goldsmiths'-Kress Library of Economic Literature and American Fiction, 1774–1910 included work with library collections and catalogues that comprised eighteenth-century books (Meckler, 1982: 96, 93).

---

[9] In 1995 RPI was renamed Primary Source Media, which also traded under the name Primary Source Microfilm (De Mowbray, 2019c).

Alston estimated that the filming of the 18thC STC would 'take fifteen years to complete' (Alston, 1981b: 2). In fact, filming took approximately twenty-eight years between 1982 and 2010 when the programme stopped, and even then, did not manage to film everything in the ongoing and massive cataloguing programme of what was by then called the English Short Title Catalogue (de Mowbray, 2020a). Alston also envisaged that the bulk of the filming programme would be based on British Library holdings, and so the operation required the secure transportation of hundreds of thousands of eighteenth-century books to and from the British Library in London to RPI's UK offices in Reading, where filming was monitored by visiting British Library librarians (Alston, 2004; Bankoski & de Mowbray, 2019). The eventual programme would entail filming at many libraries outside the United Kingdom.

The collection was arranged into subject headings and comprised eight categories. These subject headings may well have had their origin in Alston's experiments with the 18thC STC's initial online interface at the British Library, which he felt could 'help in the creation of subject packages which will form the basis of the RPI program to microfilm the substantive texts in ESTC' (Alston, 2004). The legacy of this arrangement can be seen in the interfaces of the ECCO and Jisc Historical Texts collections, which can both still be searched by these very same categories:

Religion and Philosophy
Literature and Language
History and Geography
Fine Arts and Antiquities
Social Science
Science, Technology, and Medicine
Law (Criminal, National, and International)
General Reference and Miscellaneous

Each reel of 35 mm film was devoted to books from one category. Research Publications sold the collection either in 'units', each comprising thirty-five reels, or by subject heading, or the complete collection. In 1994 the complete collection, at that point comprising 178 units, cost £341,760; each unit of thirty-five reels cost £1,920. Individual reels could be bought for £55 or £70 each depending on the total quantity ordered at one time. Given this was a major investment for most libraries, RPI offered ways of ameliorating up-front costs: libraries who took out a standing order of a minimum of one unit per year could obtain a discount and customers could also take out an annual subscription for future units (Research Publications, 1994).

The first films were produced in 1982. While filming rates varied depending on the site, by 1986 it was estimated that books were being filmed at a rate of around 50,000 pages per week at the British Library (De Mowbray, 2019b). By 1993 RPI had published 6,230 reels and was producing '16 units a year' – that is, 560 reels (Research Publications, 1994). By 2007 the collection was 'expected to contain over 200,000 items', and by the time filming stopped in 2010 the collection amounted to 18,094 reels.[10]

From the beginning the scale of the microfilming programme was a challenge. Given the huge amount of printed material in the period, Alston envisioned that the microfilming of the 18thC STC would be different from UMI's pre-1700 collection, Early English Books, in which 'no selection was involved, and every discrete item benefitting from an entry number was, and still is being filmed. This approach could not possibly have been adopted for ESTC: indeed, one pauses to wonder whether libraries (or scholars for that matter) have been significantly helped by the provision of whole-text filming for variants, re-impressions and re-issues, especially when set against the ever-rising costs of production' (Alston, 1981b: 2).

Alston proposed that the 18thC STC programme should be 'selective', in contrast to the apparent bibliographical promiscuity of UMI's microfilming (Alston, 1981b: 2). This policy would change, but at least with the first phase of filming, this vision seems to have been partly carried out. The 'Research Tools' section of ECCO's original interface outlines this part of its microfilm history:

[10] Primary Source Media – Eighteenth Century, http://microformguides.gale .com/BrowseGuide.asp?colldocid=2019000&Item=&Page=5; Primary Source Media – Eighteenth Century – Collection Information, http://microformguides .gale.com/Data/Introductions/20190FM.htm [accessed 26 July 2019].

Guided by the interests of those studying the texts, items initially included were limited to first and significant editions of each title. Exceptions to this rule are the works of 28 major authors, all of whose editions are included where available:

Addison, Bentham, Bishop Berkeley, Boswell, Burke, Burns, Congreve, Defoe, Jonathan Edwards, Fielding, Franklin, Garrick, Gibbon, Goldsmith, Hume, Johnson, Paine, Pope, Reynolds, Richardson, Bolingbroke, Sheridan, Adam Smith, Smollett, Steele, Sterne, Swift and Wesley.[11]

The selection is also an illuminating reflection of who was considered worthy of having *all* editions of their work microfilmed: in 1982 the scholarly perception of the canon of eighteenth-century 'major authors' included no women writers or persons of colour.

In May 1987 RPI announced in a newsletter to subscribers that it would be expanding its filming programme 'to enrich the potential for research and study offered by the microfilm collection'. The announcement gives a sense of the scale of the new filming programme, expanding enormously beyond Alston's initial vision: from 1988 'the selection criteria will be extended to include all distinct editions of a work insofar as the ESTC bibliographical record makes possible' (Research Publications, 1987). A 1994 brochure added that the collection also includes 'variant and pirated editions' (Research Publications, 1994).

The 1987 announcement is also fascinating since it reveals how RPI identified and responded to a particular shift in scholarship:

Today there is clearly a growing interest on the part of scholars in a number of fields concerning the impact of the total output of the printing press on social history. At least five international

---

[11] Gale, ECCO, Research Tools, Eighteenth Century Collections Online: Origins and Contexts, http://find.gale.com.bathspa.idm.oclc.org/ecco/researchTools [accessed 11 March 2020]. See also Primary Source Media – Eighteenth Century – Collection Information, http://microformguides.gale.com/Data/Introductions/20190FM.htm [accessed 26 July 2019].

> congresses on the history of the book and printing have been
> held recently in places as far apart as Athens, Greece and
> Boston, U.S.A. Centres for the study of the book have been
> established in such places as Wolfenbuttel, Germany,
> Washington, D.C., U.S.A. and Worcester, U.S.A.
> Distinguished scholars everywhere are making more and
> more of an effort to understand this comparatively neglected
> area of history. It is generally recognized that in order to do
> this, it is necessary to have access to the actual books that were
> produced through printing. (Research Publications, 1987)

Research Publications strategically positioned its decision in relation to the
rise of studies in the history of the book, arguably attributable to the
influence of the *Histoire du Livre* of the 1980s led by Roger Chartier and
Robert Darnton. Research Publications' argument rests on the implication
that bibliographical records are insufficient on their own: you need access to
the 'actual books'. This is perfectly right, of course; certain aspects of book
history and bibliography require the analysis of the physical book.
However, RPI's announcement was artful marketing: while the collection
certainly enabled access to a version of a book, the collection could not offer
access to a physical book.

Research Publications' 1994 brochure draws on a similar discourse:

> Here is the opportunity to study original primary source
> material from around the world without the time and expense
> of travel. We have preserved unique documents and rare
> books in a time-saving, cost-effective format. Now you can
> have easy access to the printed books, pamphlets and docu-
> ments that were actually used during the eighteenth century.

As in Power's and Binkley's visions of the 1930s, access to rare research
documents was the defining advantage to microfilm. Research Publications'
brochure echoes this affordance, claiming it 'will bring a comprehensive
rare book archive to your library', as if delivering a research library to your
doorstep. Like it had in its newsletter of 1987, RPI trumpets the collection's

Figure 5 Microfilm reader and author's laptop, British Library, 2019

ability to aid the scholar interested in the history of the book and in bibliography: 'Literary scholars can make textual comparisons between variant editions of many works' and can 'investigate the mysteries of false imprints or examine the printing history of a particular work' (Research Publications, 1994). This is true to an extent, but as we will see in 'Bookishness', some mysteries need more than a flat, two-dimensional representation of a book to be unlocked.

Access, however, is inextricable from the experience of *how* a particular technology of remediation is used, and there was a glaring disparity between the commercial praise of the medium and the physical experience of using the technology. It involved fiddling with reels and threading film, then shuttling through the items on each film to find the book you wanted (by hand-crank or motor power); even then, the image could often be marred by poor lighting. I feel the pain of a reader in 1940 who remarked, 'reading by means of a mechanical contrivance is so new and so unprecedented in the entire history of writing and printing that it introduces, in addition to its real and obvious difficulties, those of a psychological nature on the part of the prospective reader' (quoted in Meckler, 1982: 60). As an interface to old books the microfilm reader was not user-friendly.

Against the reality of microfilm use, the methods of reproduction promoted by libraries and publishers conjured an image of an easily and immediately navigable landscape of books and information. This is nicely captured in a 1979 study of microform publishing that ends with a vision of the future in which a car would have a microfiche viewer instead of using printed road maps, presumably using one while stationary (Ashby & Campbell, 1979: 170–1). The future is here, these studies seem to be saying: witness the title of a study published in 2000 – *Micrographics: Technology for the 21st Century* (Saffedy, 2000). Saffedy's book, to be fair, concludes by considering the impact of digitisation and computers. He proposes a system whereby the use of microfilm collections might be synthesised with 'electronic document imaging systems' and 'database management software'. Perhaps unconsciously echoing Vannevar Bush's 'Memex', Saffedy imagines 'retrieval stations' that would comprise a mix of computers for images and database searches and microfilm reader-printers (Saffedy, 2000: 120). Such an experience was clearly in the mind of Robin Alston when, in his announcement for the microfilming of the 18thC STC, he anticipated that the users could navigate between online access to electronic records and microfilmed images of eighteenth-century books (Alston, 1981b: 2). His hopes echo the kind of utopianism of Binkley: that technology would enable not only access to rare texts, but also a way of *practising* scholarship. But how might this practice work when it comes to the study of an actual book from the eighteenth century, navigating between book, catalogue record, and filmed and digitised image?

3 Bookishness

When I was examining the 1756 copy of Patrick Browne's *The Civil and Natural History of Jamaica* in the British Library as part of my case study research, I was struck by the sheer physicality of this book. It was big and heavy and the paper was thick – I had to heave it onto the table, and I could feel the stiffness of the pages as I turned them. Yet despite the book's heft, I had to be quite careful in opening up its large map of Jamaica (Figure 6). While we sometimes forget this, we always encounter the printed book physically, but this book's shape imposed itself on me, reminding me that reading is a material experience, 'an engagement with the body', as Roger Chartier put it (quoted in Nunberg, 1993: 17). Partly for fun, but partly because I couldn't find a suitable single word to describe this materiality, I use the term 'bookishness'.[12]

Thinking about bookishness enables us to explore how the reproduction of an old book as a record, or as a microfilm, or as digital images radically alters the possibilities of scholarship but also amplifies the limits by which we

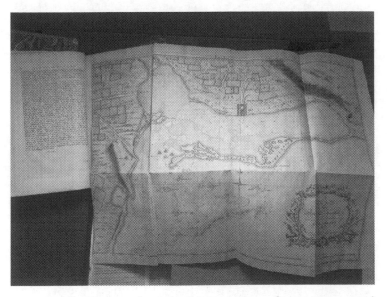

Figure 6 Opened map in *The Civil and Natural History of Jamaica*, 1756, British Library

---

[12] See OED, 'Bookish': 2: 'Of or belonging to a book or books'.

can apprehend this materiality, this bookishness. This section in short asks: what are the traces of bookishness in a catalogue record and a digital image?

Book, Record, and Film

In 2002 a camera operator from Primary Source Microfilms arrived at the Kenneth Spencer Library of Kansas University to begin filming books, a process which took place from late May 2002 to early February 2003 (Cook, 2019). While there, the operator filmed a 1789 copy of Patrick Browne's *The Civil and Natural History of Jamaica*. This is the story of that book and how it became a catalogue record and then photographic images, and eventually digitised in ECCO. The story aims to raise some important questions about how we read the relationship between a book's record – or its bibliographical data, to be more precise – and its digital page images. These questions illuminate the cultural and technological contexts we've examined in our prehistory of ECCO.

The Civil and Natural History of Jamaica is famous for being the first book in print by an English speaker to use the classification system created by the pioneering botanist and zoologist Carl Linnaeus (1707–78). Its existence is recorded in the English Short Title Catalogue and represented by two versions of the book: the first edition published in 1756 (ESTC T89757) and a reissue in 1789 (ESTC T89758).[13] Both the 1756 and 1789 issues were filmed as part of the expanded programme from 1988: the presence of both versions in the microfilm collection was probably assured by RPI's expanded rational to 'include all distinct editions of a work' and 'all variants' (Research Publications, 1987, 1994). The 1756 issue, according to the ESTC, was not published on film until 2005, and was a copy held in the British Library (shelfmark 459.c.4). However, the first copy of Browne's *History* that was filmed was the 1789 copy held in the Spencer Library (call number Linnaeana G13), and it was filmed and published in 2002. The note accompanying the book on the microfilm has a 'Batch date' of 10 June 2001, suggesting that the

---

[13] For a detailed bibliographical account, see E. C. Nelson (1997). An 'issue' is a variation from the original edition planned by the publisher, but with only minor differences in, for example, title page, imprint, or paper, and does not include major changes to the text of the book (Greetham, 1994: 168).

filming of the copy was planned well in advance. Without records of filming operations, it is difficult to say why this copy was filmed before the British Library copy. Possibly of interest was the library's collection of 'Linnaeana' (works associated with Carl Linnaeus) and the fact that the Spencer Library had at that point one of the largest collections of eighteenth-century material in the United States, and so it was probable that this library was made a specific target for filming and that Browne's *History* was swept up in the filming of this collection.[14]

However, the relationship between bibliographical records, this particular book copy, and its filmed and digitised copies illustrates a number of significant issues about how we read what the ESTC catalogue calls 'Surrogates'. In the ESTC entry for the 1756 edition (T89757) the 'General note' states that a 'variant has pp. 1–12 revised and reset', yet this clearly relates to the 1789 reissue. When it comes to the physical description in the ESTC catalogue for the 1789 reissue (T89758) there are a number of interesting features. This is the full description:

Physical description.
[6], viii, 503, [47]p., plates: map; 2°.[15]
General note.
With a half-title and four additional indexes. With a list of subscribers.
A reissue of the sheets of the 1756 edition, with a new titlepage.[16]

E. C. Nelson argues that, according to his research, the ESTC records are 'incorrect' (Nelson, 1997: 333, n. 9). It is true that the description of the 1789 issue does not mention features held in common by all the copies of the 1789 issue, such as the revised and reset pages, that both the 1756 and 1789 issues

---

[14] Henry Snyder, director of the US ESTC, taught at Kansas University from 1963 to 1979 so he might have been familiar with the library's collections.

[15] This is a pagination statement: it means that there are 6 unnumbered pages (in this case preliminary material), then prefatory pages in Roman numerals to viii, followed by 503 numbered pages, and then 47 unnumbered pages (in this case indexes); it also indicates that the book includes plates (in this case engravings) and a map, and finally that the book is in a folio format.

[16] Half-title: a page with just the main title and no other details.

have a misnumbered page, or the reversed engravings.[17] But Nelson misunderstands the nature of a bibliographical description in a catalogue like the ESTC. More particularly, it reveals the challenges the 'eccentric evidence' of the unique or individual book copy presents to a universal cataloguing system like MARC (Alston, 1981a: 379).

To illustrate this eccentricity, there are variations between copies of the 1789 issue itself, which a quick comparison with two other copies available via Google Books reveals. For example, the ESTC states that this issue has a 'half-title', but this element is not present in all the copies. In addition, not all copies have the map of Jamaica, and considerable differences appear in the order and presence of the preliminary material.

These variations amongst copies of the same issue of this book bear out Sarah Werner's remarks about physical descriptions in catalogues, in that they relate to an ideal copy: 'the imagined version of the book that is most perfect and complete, regardless of whether the library's copy matches it or not' (Werner, 2019: 121). In other words, no catalogue could possibly account for all the variations of all book copies held in the world. In this way the ESTC's description of T89758 is a palimpsest of all the book copies consulted. It has everything: the half-title, the list of subscribers, and the map. To press this point home, not only is the half-title missing from the copy held in the Spencer Library, but the engravings are unusually placed. Rather than being arranged in a numbered sequence towards the end of the book, which is how other copies of T89758 are arranged, in this copy the engravings are scattered throughout the book.

This alone might be enough to make the point about the differences between a record and a unique book copy. However, the book's appearance on both microfilm and ECCO even more strikingly opens up this gap between a record and a book's representation in images: nearly every page that has an engraving and an opposite page of text is duplicated. In every instance of duplication there is a faint version of the page and a more defined one. In these page images the first image was also filmed at a skewed angle (Figures 7–10).

---

[17] In the 'Preface' to Book II, Part III, p. ccclxxviii is misnumbered ccclxxix. Nelson did not notice this.

Source location	Prelims (in the order that they appear)	Other features and pagination statement
British Library	Catalogue of authors Map Dedication Preface Main body text	Half-title No list of subscribers Engravings
Kansas University Library (ECCO)	Dedication Catalogue of authors List of subscribers Preface Map Main body text	No half-title Engravings inserted throughout [6], v–viii, 503 [47]p
Library Orta Botanico di Roma (Google Books)	Preface (starts at p. v) Dedication List of subscribers Main body text	With half-title No map Catalogue of authors appears after the indexes and before engravings Engravings at end, in numeric order v–viii [4], 503 [49]p
Osterreichische Nationalbibliothek (Google Books)	Dedication Catalogue of authors Preface Map Main body text	With half-title No list of subscribers Engravings at end, in numeric order [4], v–viii, 503 [47]p

Certainly at the point of filming, moving from text to engraved images must have presented a problem in maintaining consistent image quality and contrast. In addition, books of natural history, which often incorporated illustrations and maps, some of which might have been printed on a fold-out

Figure 7 ECCO. Image no. 106

page, pose challenges to any camera operator. In this copy our camera operator had three tries at filming the fold-out map of Jamaica (two are partial images, and one manages to fit in the whole map). Less obviously, but perhaps more important in reading the text or if one is relying on 'all text' searching, is the fact that six pages are missing.[18] In any case it is clear

[18] The missing pages are 150–1, 188–9, and 302–3.

ADIANTUM 11. *Flavum ramofiſſimum, aculeatum; ramulis & frondibus tenuiſſimis.*

Adiantum *Frondibus ſupradecompoſitis, pinnis palmatis multifidis, caule aculeato.* L. Sp. pl.

Filix *Ramoſa major caule ſpinoſo, &c.* Slo. Cat. 23. & H. t. 61.

This plant is very much divided, and furniſhed with a great number of ſhort recurved prickles; its branches are very ſlender, and the leaves ſmall and deeply crenated: it grows in tufts, and is found in great abundance *Above-rocks,* and in many other parts of the Iſland.

All theſe Species of the Adiantum are light ſubaſtringent vulneraries, and may be adminiſtered with great propriety in all relaxations and weakneſſes of the fibres; in purulent conſumptions; and in the ulcerated or relaxed ſtate of the glands, eſpecially thoſe of the breaſt; as well as in moſt cutaneous diſeaſes.

S E C T.   III.

Of ſuch as have their Fructifications diſpoſed in ſimple Lines, under and along the Margin of the Sinus's, or Inciſions of the Foliage.

LONCHITIS 1. *Erecta ramoſa, pinnulis profundè crenatis.*
An, Lonchitis *Altiſſima globuligera, &c.* Pl. t. 31.
Adiantum *Nigrum ramoſum maximum, foliis ſeu pennulis obtuſis variè ſed pulcherimè ſinuatis & dentatis.* Slo. Cat. 22. & H. t. 57.

The larger Lonchitis with a ſmooth diſſected foliage.

This plant grows very common in the woods: it riſes generally to the height of three or four feet, and ſpreads a good deal in its growth: it is eaſily diſtinguiſhed by its ſmoothneſs, and the divided appearance of its foliage.

LONCHITIS 2. *Erecta tribrachiata, lateralibus tripartitis, medio recto ſimplici.* Tab. I. fig. 1, & 2.

The tripartite Lonchitis.

This plant riſes by a ſimple ſtalk to the height of two or three feet, and then divides into three parts, whereof the middle is ſimple; but each of the lateral diviſions is again parted into three ſimple branches of a proportionate length: it grows in the mountains of *New Liguanee,* and has not been obſerved by either *Plumier,* or Sir *Hans Sloan.*

LONCHITIS 3. *Hirſuta, coſta ſimpliciter pennata, lobis oblongis obtuſè crenatis.*
Lonchitis *Frondibus pinnatifidis obtuſis integerimis, ſurculis ramoſis hirſutis.* L. Sp. Pl.
Filix *Villoſa pinnulis quercinis.* Pk. t. 30. f. 3.

This plant riſes commonly to the height of four or five feet; it is moderately hirſute, and often found in the mountains of *St. Anne's.*

Figure 8 ECCO. Image no. 107

Figure 9 ECCO. Image no. 108

our camera operator was, in the words of one Kansas University librarian, 'not having a good day' (Cook, 2019). The bad day for this one operator was then replicated in the book's digitisation.[19]

---

[19] This must have taken place very soon after filming: digitisation of the first batch of texts was completed by early 2003 and the first unit of ECCO to be published – 'History and Geography' – was published in June 2003.

ADIANTUM 11. *Flavum ramofiſſimum, aculeatum; ramulis & frondibus tenuiſſimis.*

Adiantum *Frondibus ſupradecompoſitis, pinnis palmatis multifidis, cauli aculeato.* L. Sp. pl.

Filix *Ramoſa major caule ſpinoſo, &c.* Slo. Cat. 23. & H. t. 61.

This plant is very much divided, and furniſhed with a great number of ſhort recurved prickles; its branches are very ſlender, and the leaves ſmall and deeply crenated: it grows in tufts, and is found in great abundance *Above-rocks*, and in many other parts of the Iſland.

All theſe Species of the Adiantum are light ſubaſtringent vulneraries, and may be adminiſtred with great propriety in all relaxations and weakneſſes of the fibres; in purulent conſumptions; and in the ulcerated or relaxed ſtate of the glands, eſpecially thoſe of the breaſt; as well as in moſt cutaneous diſeaſes.

S E C T. III.

Of ſuch as have their Fructifications diſpoſed in ſimple Lines, under and along the Margin of the Sinus's, or Inciſions of the Foliage.

LONCHITIS 1. *Erecta ramoſa, pinnulis profundè crenatis*
An, Lonchitis *Altiſſima globuligera, &c.* Pl. t. 31.
Adiantum *Nigrum ramoſiem maximum, foliis ſeu pennulis obtuſis variè ſed pulcherimè ſinuatis & dentatis.* Slo. Cat. 22. & H. t. 57.

The larger Lonchitis with a ſmooth diſſected foliage.

This plant grows very common in the woods: it riſes generally to the height of three or four feet, and ſpreads a good deal in its growth: it is eaſily diſtinguiſhed by its ſmoothneſs, and the divided appearance of its foliage.

LONCHITIS 2. *Erecta tribrachiata, lateralibus tripartitis, medio recta ſimplici.* Tab. I. fig. 1, & 2.

The tripartite Lonchitis.

This plant riſes by a ſimple ſtalk to the height of two or three feet, and then divides into three parts, whereof the middle is ſimple; but each of the lateral diviſions is again parted into three ſimple branches of a proportionate length: it grows in the mountains of *New Liguance*, and has not been obſerved by either *Plumier*, or Sir *Hans Sloan*.

LONCHITIS 3. *Hirſuta, coſta ſimpliciter pennata, lobis oblongis obtuſè crenatis.*
Lonchitis *Frondibus pinnatifidis obtuſis integerimis, ſurculis ramoſis birſutis.* L. Sp. Pl.
Filix *Villoſa pinnulis quercinis.* Pk. t. 30. f. 3.

This plant riſes commonly to the height of four or five feet, it is moderately birſute, and often found in the mountains of *St. Anne's*.

Figure 10 ECCO. Image no. 109

This finally leads us to consider the refracted relationship between a bibliographical record and an image of a specific book copy. Alston hoped that readers could navigate between these and, to an extent, this was realised in ECCO interfaces where users can pull up bibliographic metadata alongside page images. However, there is an essential tension between the record and the book. Using either the record or the filmed image to read a particular significance into the order of the preliminary material, or into the relationship between the place of the engraved images and the corresponding text, is to confuse the ideal with the material, or the general record with the particular book that was filmed and digitised for ECCO. Michael Gavin has argued that such warnings from scholars are projections of '(presumably superseded) naiveté onto the digital project they wished to critique' (Gavin, 2019: 74, n. 5). Gavin, however, presumes a bibliographical knowledge that many humanities students do not possess. Gale never made any claim that individual book images represent the messy, material vagaries of every hand-press book copy in their collections (though EEBO did at one point; see Gadd, 2009). However, without some understanding of cataloguing systems, the book in the hand-press era, or the processes involved in the remediation of a book copy, that pitfall exists for the unschooled user.

The aim of this analysis is not to emphasise failings on the part of ECCO or the ESTC or even students and scholars. Instead, this reading of one book from the eighteenth century helps us to understand how human, cultural, and technological factors affect and transform our apprehension of the physical book itself, its bookishness.

Bookishness and the Digital Image

This is a good moment to exemplify how the processes of microfilming interact with the next stage in our books' lives: the digitisation of the microfilm collection. How we see and conceive these books as digital images in ECCO is to a significant degree dependent on decisions made by RPI/Primary Source Media during the filming programme and by Gale during the digitisation of the film images: these in turn shape our apprehension of these books' bookishness.

One decision made during the filming of the 18thC STC has profound consequences for understanding these books' bookishness: no bindings or endleaves were filmed (the blank sheets of paper before and after the text). In the hand-press period these were not part of the printing process, but were the job of the binder, who would usually take direction from the book's buyer as to the type and quality of the binding. I focus here on one part of the binding, the paste-down (where one endpaper was glued to the underside of the outer binding), because the paste-down is more than merely utilitarian and can be a space for aesthetic decoration (Berger, 2019). Our example is from Charlotte Charke's autobiography, *The Narrative of Mrs Charlotte Charke*, and the source copy for ECCO's first edition of 1755 (ESTC: T68299) held in the British Library (shelfmark G.14246). On the paste-down of the *Narrative* we can see the owner's stamp as well as a curious object that seems constructed from scraps of leather bookbinding and looks like a tiny book or the spines of three books on a shelf (Figure 11).[20]

The copy belonged to Sir Thomas Grenville; if you look him up you'll find out that this politician was also a book collector, which might explain the lovely detail of a miniature book. Of course, books were sometimes bound or rebound long after the printing of the books, but nevertheless bindings and endleaves can give us important clues to significant aspects of bookishness, such as its readership or owners ('provenance'), as well as clues to the context of its production, dissemination, and use (Pearson, 2008: 93–159; Berger, 2019; Werner, 2019: 71–8, 137–8).

Another decision was to photograph books in black and white, a choice clearly based on the processing costs. Colour photography and processing would have increased costs enormously and there was understandably little benefit to be gained, given the fact that mostly all hand-press printing was done in black and white in the eighteenth century. However, it does mean that we miss the chance to see the occasional use of red ink. Compare the two images of this title page from volume one of *The Works of Alexander Pope*, 1736: one from ECCO, the other from my own copy (Figures 12–13).[21]

[20] Thanks to Ian Gadd who suggested the latter reading.

[21] In an odd twist the book you're reading is printed in black and white; the colour images can be seen in the online version.

Figure 11 Pastedown, *Narrative*

THE
WORKS

OF

ALEXANDER POPE, Esq;
VOL. I.

WITH

Explanatory NOTES and ADDITIONS
never before printed.

---

*Hæc ſtudia adoleſcentiam alunt, ſeneɛtutem obleɛtant ; ſe-
cundas res ornant, adverſis perfugium & ſolatium præ-
bent; deleɛtant domi, non impediunt foris ; pernoɛtant
nobiſcum, peregrinantur, ruſticantur.* Tully.

LONDON:

Printed for B. LINTOT, 1736.

Figure 12 *Works*. ECCO

Red ink was usually reserved for religious works and almanacs and marked off special days, but red ink was also used sometimes to pick out words on a title page. This simple decision is revealing: title pages were

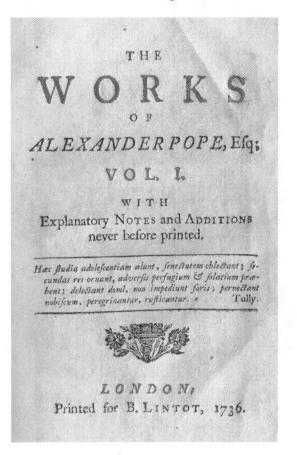

Figure 13 *Works*. Author's own copy

a form of advertisement, so red ink added to the book's visual impact, heightening the perceived value or status of the book and its author. But given it required the printer to run the sheet of paper through the printing press twice, it was costly in terms of the time and extra patience needed in the printing process: in short, the book better be worth it (Werner, 2019:

57–8). Looking at the title page from my copy of this volume of Pope's *Works*, even if we know very little about Pope, the care attending this one page might start to tell us much about either his own or his publisher's regard for the status and selling power of his works. Granted, the ESTC records the fact that the title page is in red and black and this bibliographic metadata is available in the original ECCO interface and the Gale Primary Sources interface, but we'd have to guess which words since that detail is not recorded. All this most certainly would be lost if we only depended upon the microfilm or the image in ECCO.

It is not just colour that is lost by microfilming. In 1941, in the early years of microfilming old books, William Jackson objected to what I could call the two-dimensionality of film images of books, saying, 'it is a photograph taken ... in one plane', and adding that the reader can't benefit from 'raking' light (Jackson, 1941: 283). More recently, Sarah Werner made the point that raking light during digital imaging can bring alive the material texture of old books (Werner, 2012). The example I use is again *The Narrative of Mrs Charlotte Charke*, but this time the second edition of 1755 (ESTC T68298), ECCO's source copy in the British Library (shelf-mark C.184.b.16). In both editions of 1755 the format of the book was duodecimo (12°), a popular, small, and relatively portable format. However, this particular copy is strikingly different: in addition to the printed text of her *Narrative*, throughout the book are interspersed playbills and newspaper cuttings (Figures 14–15), and there is a lot of blank space around some of the text.

Why is it like this and how was it made? The high-contrast two-dimensionality of the filmed page images in ECCO does not afford the kind of detail that might help. My own photograph of the title page, taken in raking light and from an angle, I hope, reveals more about the book's construction (Figure 16).

The edge of 'original' printed text is visibly different from the larger-size paper upon which it is mounted. This is a good piece of evidence that we are looking at an example of scrapbooking, where a book owner has collected this miscellaneous material related to Charke's life and had it interleaved with the printed text of Charke's autobiography in a book of a much larger format (one of my students called this owner a 'super fan' of Charke's).

(a)   (b)

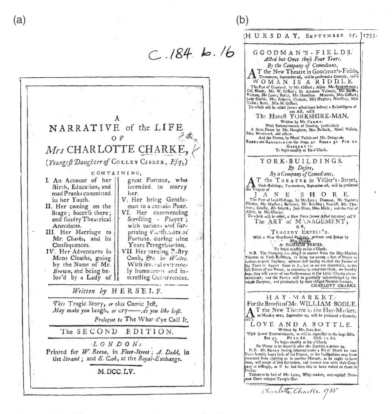

Figure 14 Title page, *Narrative*, second edition. ECCO

Double lines appear around the printed text (are these hand-drawn?), and a fainter impression emerges outside these lines (what made this?). Answers to these questions might provide valuable bookish clues as to how it was made, the role of the binder and owner in its construction, and perhaps even how it was used and valued.

Another aspect of bookishness affected by filming and digitisation is the experience of reading an *open* book. Typically, camera operators for RPI/ Primary Source Media would film the books depending upon their size or

THURSDAY, September 25, 1735.

GOODMAN'S - FIELDS.
Acted but Once these Four Years.
By the Company of Comedians,
AT the New Theatre in Goodman's-Fields,
To-morrow, September 26, will be presented a Comedy, call'd
WOMAN IS A RIDDLE.
The Part of Courtwell, by Mr. Giffard; Aspin, Mr. Penkethman;
Col. Manly, Mr. W. Giffard; Sir Amorous Vainwit, Mr. Bardin;
Vulture, Mr. Lyon; Butler, Mr. Hamilton. Miranda, Mrs. Giffard;
Lady Outside, Mrs. Roberts; Clarinda, Miss Hughes; Necessary, Miss
Tollet; Betty, Mrs. M. Giffard.
To which will be added (never acted there before) a Ballad Opera of
one Act, call'd
The Honest YORKSHIRE-MAN.
Written by Mr. CAREY.
With Entertainments of Dancing, particularly
A Scots Dance by Mr. Haughton, Mrs. Bullock, Monf. Vallois,
Mrs. Woodward, and others.
And the Pierots, by Monf. Vallois and Mr. Delagarde.
BOXES and BALCONIES on the Stage, 4s. BOXES 3s. PIT 2s.
GALLERY 1s.
To begin exactly at Six o'Clock.

YORK-BUILDINGS.
By Desire,
By a Company of Comedians,
AT the THEATRE in Villier's - Street,
York-Buildings, To-morrow, September 26, will be presented
the Tragedy of
JANE SHORE.
The Part of Lord Hastings, by Mr. Lacy; Dumont, Mr. Turner;
Gloster, Mr. Machen; Belmour, Mr Boothby; Ratcliff, Mr. Tho-
mas; Catesby, Mr. Smyth; Jane Shore, Mrs. Male; and the Part of
Alicia, by Mrs. Charke.
To which will be added, a New Farce (never Acted but once) call'd
The ART of MANAGEMENT;
OR,
TRAGEDY EXPELL'D.
With a New Occasional Prologue, written and spoken by
Mrs. Charke.
At COMMON PRICES.
To begin exactly at Six o'Clock.
N.B. The Company are oblig'd to remove from the Hay-Market
Theatre to York-Buildings, as being too young a Sett of People to
venture at great Expences, without first having merited the Favour of
the Town to support them in it; but as we are determin'd, to the
full Extent of our Power, to endeavour to entertain them, we humbly
hope they will accept of our Performances at the Little Theatre above-
mentioned; and the Favour will be gratefully acknowledged by the
whole Company, and particularly by their obliged Humble Servant,
CHARLOTT CHARKE.

HAY-MARKET.
For the Benefit of Mr. WILLIAM BODLE.
AT the New Theatre in the Hay-Market,
on Monday next, September 29, will be presented a Comedy,
call'd
LOVE AND A BOTTLE.
Written by Mr. Farquhar.
With several Entertainments, as will be expressed in the large Bills.
Box 4s. Pit 2s. 6d. Gall. 1s. 6d.
To begin exactly at Six o'Clock.
No Money to be return'd after the Curtain is drawn up.
N.B. Mr. BODLE having laboured under a Fit of Illness for two
Years humbly hopes such of his Friends, as his Indisposition may have
prevented from applying to in another Manner, as he ought to have
done, will accept of this Invitation, and honour him with their Com-
pany as willingly, as if he had been able to have waited on them in
Person.
Tickets to be had of Mr. Lynn, Whip-maker, over-against Deve-
reux Court without Temple-Bar.

Charlotte Charke 1735

Figure 15 Second page, *Narrative*, second edition. ECCO

Figure 16 Detail of title page, *Narrative*, second edition

format.[22] The smaller book formats like duodecimo and octavo tended to be filmed two pages at a time – that is, they preserved what's known as the page spread or opening (larger sizes such folios were sometimes filmed one page at a time). As part of the processing of the films into digital image files Gale required single-page images. This processing has a number of consequences for how we see and apprehend books in ECCO.

---

[22] Information about the 'format' of a book produced in the hand-press period can give us some idea of its size, but they are not synonymous terms. 'Format' refers to how the book was printed, and the popular formats were, from the largest to the smallest: folio, quarto, octavo, and duodecimo. For example, octavo (or 8°) meant that one sheet of paper was printed with *eight* pages of text on each side, then folded and cut to produce sixteen pages of text, and so it was a relatively small format (Werner, 2019: 42–54).

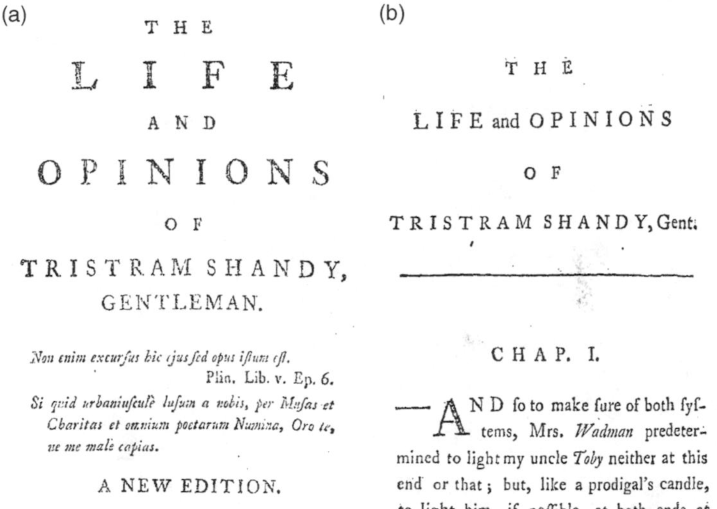

(a)

THE

L I F E

A N D

O P I N I O N S

O F

TRISTRAM SHANDY,
GENTLEMAN.

Non enim excurfus hic ejus fed opus iftum eft.
Plin. Lib. v. Ep. 6.

*Si quid urbaniufcule lufum a nobis, per Mufas et
Charitas et omnium poetarum Numina, Oro te,
ne me male capias.*

A NEW EDITION.

V O L. VI.

L O N D O N:

Printed for T. BECKET, in the Strand.
MDCCLXXV.

(b)

THE

LIFE and OPINIONS

O F

TRISTRAM SHANDY, Gent.

———————————

CHAP. I.

——— A N D fo to make fure of both fyf-
tems, Mrs. *Wadman* predeter-
mined to light my uncle *Toby* neither at this
end or that; but, like a prodigal's candle,
to light him, if poffible, at both ends at
once.

Now, through all the lumber rooms of
military furniture, including both of horfe
and foot from the great arfenal of *Venice*
VOL. VI.   B   to

Figure 17 Title page, *Tristram Shandy*. ECCO

What we're looking at now are two consecutive page images from volume
six of a 1775 edition, in octavo, of Laurence Sterne's novel, *Tristram Shandy*
as seen in ECCO (Figures 17–18).

The first page image is the title page (as we've seen, endleaves and bindings
were not filmed). Like in most book digitisations, we are invited to navigate
right to see the next page, which is the first page of chapter one. Given that in
the West we read from left to right, there is an understandable assumption
when we imagine the actual book that the title page is on the left-hand side –
the verso – and the next page is on the right – the recto. This is not actually the
case, as we can see from a photo of my own copy (Figures 19–20).

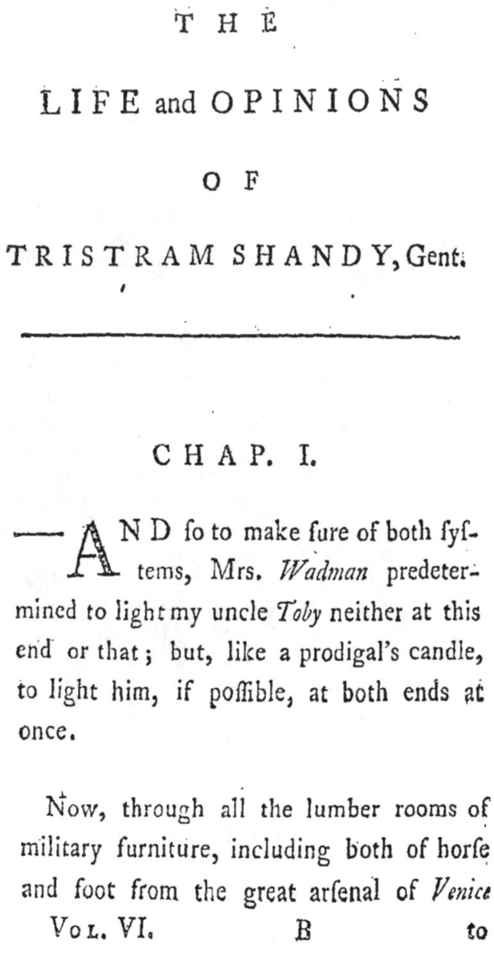

T H E

L I F E and O P I N I O N S

O F

T R I S T R A M   S H A N D Y, Gent.

C H A P. I.

—— A N D fo to make fure of both fyf-
tems, Mrs. *Wadman* predeter-
mined to light my uncle *Toby* neither at this
end or that ; but, like a prodigal's candle,
to light him, if poffible, at both ends at
once.

Now, through all the lumber rooms of
military furniture, including both of horfe
and foot from the great arfenal of *Venice*

Vol. VI.   B   to

Figure 18 Chapter page, *Tristram Shandy*. ECCO

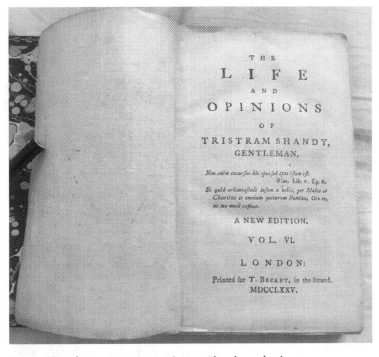

Figure 19 Title page opening, *Tristram Shandy*, author's copy

This might seem a small issue, but it matters for two reasons. First, consider that we experience a book as two pages, or opening, a 'visual unit formed by facing verso and recto pages in a codex' (Galey, 2012). The experience of reading a book in single-page units is a strange distortion of how we actually perceive the printed book as two pages. Second, the blank page opposite a first page of a chapter is not just meaningless, empty space: any printer worth their salt would be expected to give the first page of a new chapter the graphic space it needs. The decisions in digitisation have altered our apprehension of this book's bookishness.

The examples of what's happened to these books, and perhaps even the books I've chosen, might seem mundane or even unexceptional. But it is

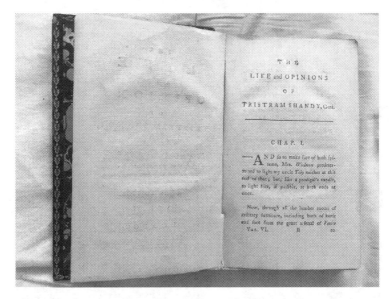

Figure 20 Chapter page opening, *Tristram Shandy*, author's copy

precisely because these examples are *not exceptional* that they are entirely
representative, and what can happen can be so easily overlooked. Moreover,
I've highlighted some of the 'losses' to a book's bookishness during these
remediations not as some kind of total critique of ECCO, but in order for us
to understand the decisions and processes in ECCO's history and so help us to
understand what we are seeing via ECCO and how we might better use this
digital archive.

4 Beginnings

Publishing, Technology, and ECCO, 1990–2004

It wasn't called ECCO at first. The original name during the project's
development in 2002 was 'The Eighteenth Century – Complete Digital
Edition', closely associating it with the microfilm collection on which it was

based (Quint, 2002). The finished product, renamed 'Eighteenth Century Collections Online', was published by Thomson Gale in 2003 and completed in 2004. It was officially launched in the United Kingdom at the British Library on 24 July followed by a reception at Dr Johnson's House, London (de Mowbray, 2019c). In the United States it premiered in early August at the thirty-fourth meeting of the American Society for Eighteenth-Century Studies (ASECS) in Los Angeles.

But let's go back a little. Thomson Gale's entry into digital publishing is a good example of the forces at work in the 1980s and 1990s that influenced the shape of commercial academic publishing. First, techno-commercial developments took place in digitisation and in electronic transmission, enabled by cheaper computing power and the rise of personal computing. Second, library budgets faced significant pressures as a result of the increasing prices of journals and the falling demand for monographs. Taken together, these technological and market contexts pushed academic publishers to diversify their product portfolios by merging companies with expertise in electronic publishing or with existing content. These commercial strategies were also a response to the explosion and spectacular failure of companies experimenting with digital platforms and electronic publishing in the 1990s – later dubbed the 'dot.com bubble' – arguably influenced by the radical business theory propounded in Bower and Christenson's essay 'Disruptive Technologies: Catching the Wave' (Bower & Christensen, 1995; Thompson, 2005: 81–110, 309–12).

The story of Thomson Gale itself starts in 1998, as the result of a merger involving the long-established company of Gale Research (founded in 1954 by Frederick Gale Ruffner and sold to Thomson in 1985), Information Access Co., and Primary Source Media: this became the Gale Group, whose new headquarters was to be in Farmington Hills (McCracken, 1998). It was a significant moment that combined three companies with particular but overlapping expertise: Gale's specialism was reference books in the humanities, sciences, and technology; Information Access Co. specialised in CD-ROMs, microfilm, and online information; Primary Source Media was formerly Research Publications (RPI), who, as we know, produced microfilm collections of rare research materials including The Eighteenth Century. As one contemporary observed, the merger was 'a move towards the electronic age and it helps to be big in this industry' (quoted in McCracken, 1998).

In contrast to the experimentation of digital companies in the mid-1990s was the more cautious strategy publishers adopted of diversifying and monetising their existing portfolio of resources by transforming them into a new medium. Former Gale CEO Dedria Bryfonski noted that their existing content formed 'the backbone of electronic products widely used today' (quoted in Enis, 2014). Thomson had decided to begin digitising its collections as early as 1996, just before the 1998 merger: its first was The Times Literary Supplement Centenary Archive, 1902–1990, published in 1999. 'Almost all our growth now is from the migration from print to digital,' as Thomson Gale's CEO Gordon Macomber pointed out in 2004 (quoted in Berry, 2004). In another 2004 interview he emphasised that the 'lion's share of our business is nonaggregated – that is, the distribution of our *proprietary* content online' (quoted in Hane, 2004). Distributing its specialised ('nonagreggated') content enabled Gale to monetise its existing ('*proprietary*') investments, of which ECCO was the prime example.

Thomson Gale was of course eager to emphasise the affordances of digitisation for its products. Singling out ECCO as the exemplar of Thomson Gale's digital products, Macomber stressed digital accessibility over print, noting that scholars 'would have had to go [to the British Library] to get access to this material' (quoted in Berry, 2004). But ECCO was promoted as more than just access; it was represented as offering a new way of learning: as Mary Mercante, vice president for marketing put it, ECCO was also about 'searchability' (quoted in Smith, 2003). Creating new markets by diversifying and transforming content also meant harnessing the unique affordances of digital technology. So what technologies of digital reproduction and publishing were available when Thomson Gale was considering digitising its collections in the late 1990s? What was the significance of these choices, and what were Thomson Gale's competitors doing with their digitisation programmes? And what does 'digitisation' even mean?

In its broadest definition digitisation is the conversion of analogue information into digital form, such as a continuously varying voltage into a series of discrete bits of information.[23] The forms of digitisation that interest us here are methods that convert text and those that convert photographic images. Text is converted to digital form by encoding each character as a binary string of zeroes and ones, a series of discrete bits of information; for example, the letter 'a' would look like this: 01000001.[24] Photography, as we've seen, has been a key media technology for the representation of old books, but while photographs represent continuous gradations and variations in tone, shade, and colour, the digital image comprises discrete bits of information that approximate the effect of continuity. Images are transformed into a grid of discrete pixels, or bitmap, with each pixel assigned a number for colour and intensity. Black-and-white, or bitonal, images are the simplest binary forms, but 8-bit or 24-bit images can encode huge numbers of colours.

Thomson Gale began thinking about digitising its existing collections in 1996, and anyone contemplating digitising old books in the 1990s had a number of technological and commercial decisions to make. They would have to decide whether to transform the material into page images, or to produce it as searchable text, or to offer both: this would depend on the nature of the content, on who their users were, how they were expected to use it, and costs. If searchable text was on the cards, then they would need to decide between two options: to either have each word transcribed by hand (accurate but costly), or to use text automatically generated from page images using software (cheaper, but inaccurate, especially if the content was microfilm). In parallel, there were also decisions to make about how to publish the material: was it to be on CD-ROMs, or would it be online via the nascent World Wide Web?

Humanities computing had a history going back to Roberto Busa's work in the late 1940s, and digitisation projects had been running since Project Gutenberg's first electronic transcription in 1971 (Hockey, 2004; Deegan & Sutherland, 2009: 119–54; Johnston, 2012; Thylstrup, 2018: 1–31). However, Thomson Gale's attention in the 1990s was fixed on its immediate

---

[23] The first recorded use of this meaning was in 1956 (OED).

[24] The current standard is 8-bit encoding (UTF-8), as here. The first standard was ASCII, using 7 bits.

competitors in the commercial market for educational and academic resources; its engagement with the scholarly field that became known as 'Digital Humanities' did not become significant until the 2010s. Google Books, of course, was perhaps the most high-profile mass digitisation project, and was launched at the Frankfurt Book Fair in 2004. The extent to which Thomson Gale knew about Google Books while developing ECCO is not clear, but it's revealing that in 2004 CEO Macomber chose to characterise Google as an information search-and-retrieval business. Commenting on the 'challenge ... laid before us by Google and Yahoo! and others that dominate the Internet space', he argued that:

> the end user today has a lot of options to get information. The difference is that a company like Thomson Gale has a lot of phenomenal content that can upgrade the learning experience for a student or scholar ... I would characterize Thomson Gale a bit differently than an aggregator ... we think the end users' needs and wants are much more than just to search and retrieve information. We think end users need to experience differentiated content that helps to teach them what they need to learn. That is the business we are in, whether it's through print or online distribution of our content. Our content is not so much informational as it is a tool to help users learn. (Macomber, quoted in Hane, 2004)

Gale explicitly positioned itself by describing what it offers as 'differentiated content' – such as digitised book collections – and a 'tool to help users learn' in opposition to the mere aggregation of information by platforms like Yahoo! and Google.

The more immediate models for ECCO were digital products developed by Thomson Gale's peers and competitors in academic publishing, so the rest of this section looks at two examples: ProQuest's Early English Books Online (EEBO) and Chadwyck-Healey's English Poetry Full-Text Database; both are from the 1990s but model different technological and publishing choices. In the 1980s and 1990s, in addition to microfilm and the Internet, there was another publishing technology:

the CD-ROM. An adaptation of the compact audio disc, the CD-ROM (compact disc – read only memory) was designed in 1982 as a storage medium for data. Many of the microform and information publishers adopted the CD-ROM format as a way of distributing electronic resources in the 1980s and 1990s, including Gale and Primary Source Media, and even after the advent of interconnected networks of computers the CD-ROM was considered superior to the slow download speeds and expensive connection costs of the early Internet. Its high memory capacity and multimedia capabilities made it an attractive medium for a variety of resources. For example, the 18thC STC project felt that since it 'had pioneered the automation of rare books cataloguing . . . compact disc (CD-ROM) was therefore an attractive and appropriate medium' (*Factotum*, no. 30, 1989: 3).[25]

The CD-ROM, therefore, was an interesting transitional publishing medium. A case in point was Chadwyck-Healey's pioneering English Poetry Full-Text Database, published 1992–4. As Chadwyck-Healey relates, the sheer scale of the project was unprecedented: 165,000 poems. 'We were to turn all of English poetry into one huge, fully searchable database' (Chadwyck-Healey, 2020: 231, 217). To enable the user to search for authors, titles, or first lines, every single poem had to be transcribed and encoded by hand in order to accurately render particular elements of each poem. Eventually, Chadwyck-Healey published nine different literary databases this way (Thompson, 2005: 395). However, the English Poetry package illuminates some of the oddities of CD-ROM publications. On one hand, the ability to conduct searches across the landscape of English poetry demonstrates a crucial affordance of electronically transcribed text. However, the package of disks, software disks, a manual, and a printed bibliography created limitations on its user friendliness. Moreover, the CD-ROM could not meet libraries' demand to enable multiple users to simultaneously access resources (it could only be used by one person at a time), and it was hampered by both proprietary software and hardware requirements that were often out of date within a few years.

---

[25] It was published on CD-ROM in 1992. *Factotum*, no. 35, August 1992, p. 3.

Chadwyck-Healey ruefully acknowledged that 'in less than ten years, the CD-ROM revolution was over' (Chadwyck-Healey, 2020: 260). The CD-ROM represented a form of technology in a state of short-lived infancy: online, networked, and web-based publications were fast becoming the future of academic digitisation products. Networked, multiple-user access, and the ability to update and tailor specific packages for libraries were attractive advantages. Chadwyck-Healey, for example, had to create business cases based on a model of sharing information that was, on the surface, free via the Internet. The answer was an annual subscription charge for access to a resource, as opposed to a library owning it, and Chadwyck-Healey launched Literature Online (LION) in 1996 (Thompson, 2005: 394–9; Chadwyck-Healey, 2020: 261–3). This business model was one that companies like ProQuest and Gale quickly adopted.

ProQuest's Early English Books Online (EEBO) was published as an online resource in 1998 and now comprises 146,000 titles from the period *c.*1475–1700. In terms of its source material – books from the hand-press era that had been microfilmed – it is similar to ECCO. Early English Books Online was the digitisation of UMI's original microfilm collection, Early English Books (which began with Eugene Power's filming operation in the 1930s), and was largely based on the two seminal Short Title Catalogues of printed material from *c.*1475 to 1700 created in the early twentieth century.[26] ProQuest had begun to digitise the films in 1998 as black-and-white or bitonal images, and later began processing them in greyscale in order to maximise fidelity to the printed original, although as Mak has pointed out, and as we have seen in our bookish vignettes, the emphasis on digital processing potentially 'elides the key intermediary of microfilm' (Mak, 2014: 1519). Equally interesting as its claim of fidelity was ProQuest's decision to offer just page images: there was no attempt to use OCR software to generate text from the images. In 1994 UMI were developing its own OCR software, but felt that good-quality OCR of microfilm was twenty to twenty-four months away and still too expensive (Schonfeld, 2003: 42–3). Indeed, the massive JSTOR project to digitise academic

---

[26] Gadd (2009) and Mak (2014: 1516–18) explore the complex and at times incoherent relationship between EEBO and the ESTC.

journals, developed in 1994, reveals parallel concerns. The CD-ROM limited access, and so JSTOR opted for online full-text searchability. Hand transcriptions were costly, but given the limitations of OCR software at that moment, the project opted to scan the paper originals (Schonfeld, 2003: 11–14, 28–30, 72–3). In response to the perception that EEBO 'was not quite utilizing all of the potential that electronic technology had to offer', the University of Michigan Library stepped in to form the Text Creation Partnership (TCP), a remarkable collaborative project that included ProQuest, the University of Oxford Bodleian libraries, and the Council on Library and Information Resources (Martin, 2007: 161). The project aimed to produce text that was accurate, accessible, and reusable: in the chapter 'Interfacing', we see how the TCP worked with ECCO, but its initial effect was to enable the kind of full-text searchability EEBO's original digitisation lacked.[27]

It is significant that Thomson Gale chose to make the technology of ECCO's searchability a key selling point – and also its scale – since it viewed ProQuest's EEBO as its key competitor, despite the fact that it offered material from a different period (Bankoski, 2019c). Clearly, by 2000 when the ECCO project began, Thomson Gale felt that the cost-benefits of using OCR software on microfilm were in its favour. As the writer of a document entitled 'ECCO Prototype Walk-Through' noted, full-text searching was 'a MAJOR feature as it searches the full 29 million pages in ECCO; also not available in EEBO' (unpublished, c.2003; emphasis in the original). Gale was certainly keen to talk up the potential of combining searchability with scale. The 2004 User's Guide described it this way:

> *Eighteenth Century Collections Online* (ECCO) is a comprehensive digital archive derived from *The Eighteenth Century*, the world's largest library of the printed book on microfilm, available through Gale's imprint, Primary Source Microfilm™. In the most ambitious single digitization project

---

[27] Text Creation Partnership – About the Partnership, https://textcreationpart nership.org/about-the-tcp/ [accessed 4 January 2020].

ever undertaken, nearly 150,000 volumes of English language
works and editions published during the eighteenth century are
being made available online, ready to explore using Gale's
powerful and familiar search interface. *ECCO* features nearly
30 million pages of material; in essence, every significant
English-language and foreign language title printed in the
United Kingdom, along with thousands of important works
from the Americas, Europe and the Empire. (Gale, 2004: 4)

ProQuest's EEBO comprised 125,000 titles at its launch in 1998: Thomson
Gale's emphasis on the size of ECCO was certainly with its competitors in
mind.[28]

Scale and technology cost money: one scholar described it as 'this
quarter-million-dollar investment' (Garrett, 2007: 71). Given this, and the
fact that ECCO was to be an online product, Thomson Gale's sales strategy
was to offer ECCO as both a product and a subscription. There was a one-
off payment for the content and a yearly hosting or access fee: libraries who
bought the content could theoretically host the content on their own servers
and interface, but no library has yet gone down that route. Reviewers at the
time quoted a list price of $500,000 or £315,000 for the complete collection,
although ECCO could be bought on a unit-by-unit basis, following the
same categories that grouped the microfilm collection, which meant that
institutions could buy individual units or spread the cost over time (Levack,
2003; Schwarz, 2004). In addition, Gale offered discounted prices for
institutions that had bought its microfilm collection (Smith, 2003).

Thomson Gale, therefore, was navigating between costs, existing technological developments, the nature of the original material, the needs of its
market, and its competitors. 'We own the 18th century'; so proclaimed
Mark Holland, a UK representative from Thomson Gale (quoted in Quint,
2002). In one sense, this comment reflected Thomson Gale's literal owner-
ship of the film collection, but in its confident aggrandisement it spoke

---

[28] Note the careful claim that ECCO includes 'every *significant* . . . title' (my
emphasis): it does not represent the entirety of the print record of the period.

volumes about Thomson Gale's ambition to be the one publisher everyone goes to for eighteenth-century research materials.

From Film Image to Metadata: Digitising the Eighteenth Century
Against this background, then, Thomson Gale aimed to create a new market for its content by combining the long-standing bibliographic sentiment of access to old books with the informatic sensibility shaping the online world. The following section explores the three aspects of the books in ECCO: the digital page image, the OCR text, and finally the metadata upon which the interface's search functions depend.

The digitisation of the microfilm collection began in 2000 (Bankoski, 2019a).[29] This was while the programme of microfilming eighteenth-century books was still going, and while the film collection was still being published (filming stopped in 2010). This explains why Gale published a second collection called ECCO II in 2009 of an additional 46,000 or so extra titles: in effect, a scanning programme that caught up with some of the microfilming done between 2003 and 2009.[30] Gale contracted the digitisation of the microfilm to HTC Global, an IT services company founded in 1990, and whose headquarters is in Troy, Michigan. HTC has offices across the globe, but the microfilms of The Eighteenth Century were shipped out to India for processing. Natraj Kumar, in charge of the operation in India, estimates that nearly 500 people were involved in the two-year digitisation, including more than 350 production operatives, more than 100 on quality control, and 75 in supporting service roles (Kumar, 2019). According to Ray Bankoski, the vice president of content and metadata at Gale, most of these workers 'were keying and QC operators that captured the metadata from the page images. There was an initial ramp up period but we processed about 500 K [page images] per week over the majority of the two year period' (Bankoski, 2019a).

---

[29] An early review incorrectly claims that ECCO was 'first conceptualized in the fall of 2002 and was essentially developed within nine months'; this probably refers to the development of the interface (Levack, 2003: 37).

[30] In 2020 Gale began a new programme of digitising eighteenth-century books to be published as ECCO III.

The actual conversion of the reels of film images to digital files was accomplished by a Sunrise Model 2000+ scanner and then processed in various ways (Kumar, 2019). Typically, microfilming meant photographing a double-page spread or 'opening', except in the case of large-format books or books with big or fold-out maps and illustrations where single pages were photographed individually. However, when these were digitised the images were processed into single pages: this was a 'requirement from Gale at that time. Gale wanted "Clean cropped Page Images" to be delivered' (Kumar, 2019). In addition, films were digitised as bitonal images. These decisions likely helped to produce page images with fewer extraneous marks and a high contrast between the black text and the white page, and therefore aided the OCR software to decode the text. As we've seen, the effect on how printed material looks is significant.

Page images were saved as tagged image file format (TIFF) files. This file format was developed in the late 1980s as a standard for storing raster graphics or bitmaps so that digitised images can be easily converted into pixels on the computer screen. For users who want to download page images to their own computers the files are made available as portable document files (PDFs). The PDF was designed in the early 1990s in order to create 'a universal way to communicate documents' and 'should be viewable on any display and should be printable on any modern printers' (Warnock, 1991). Developed as part of the desktop publishing revolution that paralleled the arrival of the personal computer, this format has a wider significance in that it is a continuation of the longer history of reproducing books as images: they 'look as if they work like print', as Lisa Gitelman argues. Its 'portability' aimed to ensure that the image looks the same whether on screen or in print. In this sense, the PDF 'appeals to the fixity of print' (Gitelman, 2014: 114, 118). Such an imaginary materiality would have been a natural fit for databases of old books like ECCO. Project Camelot had even imagined when '[l]arge centrally maintained databases of documents could be accessed remotely and selectively printed remotely' (Warnock, 1991). This was one of those instances when the social changes wrought by personal computing and the commercial and technological standards developed to meet those demands in the 1990s are part of the reason why old books look the way they do on databases like ECCO. However, the relatively large size of image files (compared to text files) and the limited bandwidth of the early Internet posed certain limitations on the user experience.[31] The concern was, as Julia de Mowbray put it, 'that a higher page count would adversely hit the performance and speed of the product' (de Mowbray, 2020a). At its launch in 2003 users were allowed to download only 10 pages at a time; by 2008 this had increased to 50. In 2009 the download capacity was increased to batches of 250 pages at a time (Golderman & Connolly, 2008: 25; de Mowbray, 2020a).[32]

Gale had more in mind for its users than merely downloading and printing off a few pages of, say, the first edition of *Robinson Crusoe* as a PDF file. Gale wanted to bring the kind of functionality enabled by converting images of its books into searchable text using OCR software. But how does OCR work? Image file formats are opaque to the computer: they cannot be searched for text since they are designed to enable a computer to render that encoded image on a screen. Optical character recognition software effectively scans the image files to 'read' the text of each page and convert it into a text file. Optical character recognition technology was first developed in the 1950s, although until the development of cheap powerful computing in the 1990s, it was quite limited in its abilities (Tanner et al., 2009). The OCR conversion process involves several steps. The OCR engine first preprocesses images by making sure the page is aligned correctly and the lines of words are horizontal. It then divides the page into zones, identifying blocks of text such as paragraphs, lines, and words. It then divides these blocks up again to find individual characters. It is perhaps for this reason that the creators of digitisation projects like Gale's ECCO chose to very closely crop microfilm images into single pages, avoiding the possibility that the OCR engine might mistake stray marks or a page edge for a text block or a character. 'Once the characters have been singled out', as Rose Holley describes it, 'the program compares them with a set of pattern images stored in its database. It analyzes the stroke edge, the line of discontinuity between the text

---

[31] This was an early issue for JSTOR (Schonfeld, 2003: 252–55).

[32] Gale Primary Sources and Gale Digital Scholar Lab have no download limit.

characters, and the background. Allowing for irregularities of printed ink on paper, each algorithm averages the light and dark along the side of a stroke, and advances numerous hypotheses about what this character is. Finally, the software makes a best guess decision on the character' (Holley, 2009).

The OCR engine then compares all the characters in a word block to its dictionary of complete words. The text for ECCO phase I material was produced using an OCR engine called PrimeRecognition, which used several different OCR engines operating at the same time with a voting system choosing the best character recognition. For the texts of ECCO phase II, published in 2009, Gale upgraded the OCR engine to ABBYY (Bankoski, 2020).[33]

Gale's original interface for ECCO, like Google Books, showed only page images, and not the completed text output from the OCR engine. If the user searches for a word, how then does this lead them to see the results on a page image? This necessitates a further step: each word is given a specific coordinate so that it matches the location of the word on the page image. These coordinates and the OCR text output are stored in XML format. The example that follows is the first line from Daniel Defoe's *An Essay on the Regulation of the Press* (1704):

```
<wd pos="226,548,290,588">LL</wd>
<wd pos="308,547,393,587">Men</wd>
<wd pos="414,540,561,596">pretend</wd>
 <wd pos="589,540,651,586">the</wd>
 <wd pos="675,537,949,586">Licentiousness</wd>
<wd pos="962,537,1016,585">.of</wd>
<wd pos="1033,538,1097,583">the</wd>
<wd pos="1072,523,1113,596">:,</wd>
 <wd pos="250,599,346,641">Press</wd>
 <wd pos="363,605,402,640">to</wd>
 <wd pos="423,597,469,638">be</wd>
```

[33] PrimeRecognition – PrimeOCR, https://primerecognition.com/ocr-software/ [accessed 3 January 2020]; ABBYY – OCR Process, www.abbyy.com/en-gb/ocr-sdk/ocr-stages/ [accessed 10 March 2020].

```
<wd pos="495,606,516,639">a</wd>
<wd pos="544,593,689,647">publick</wd>
<wd pos="702,591,914,642">Grievance, .</wd>
```

EXtensible Markup Language (XML) was first designed in 1996 as a way of describing, structuring, and distributing data that was not dependent on an inflexible set of rules (therefore 'extensible'); it was both human- and machine-readable, and it was not dependent on any particular software. The XML format was adopted and recommended by the World Wide Web Consortium (W3C) in 1998: HTC and Gale, then, were adopting the latest standards for structuring data for the Web. The XML file for each volume or title in ECCO also contains bibliographical metadata found in the ESTC, such as details of the author, the full title, notes about its physical make-up, the library in which the source-copy is held as well as a list of libraries where other copies are held.[34] The XML file also includes other data for each page:

```
<page type="bodyPage" firstPage="yes">
<pageInfo>
<pageID>00030</pageID>
<assetID>3304394388</assetID>
<ocrLanguage>English</ocrLanguage>
<sourcePage>3</sourcePage>
<ocr>89.1</ocr>
<imageLink pageIndicator="single" width="1184"
height="2080" type="tiff" colorimage="bito-
nal">014720280000030.TIF</imageLink>
<!-image src="065600_2.tif" ->
</pageInfo>
```

This extract from the *Essay*'s file includes various identification numbers for Gale's internal management and the link to the TIFF page image, as well as details about the image resolution (in pixels) and type (bitonal), and a figure that represents the OCR confidence for each page of text (89.1 per cent in

---

[34] The XML file is not available via ECCO interfaces.

our example). Note that this is only a measure of its recognition confidence, not a percentage of how many characters are accurate.[35]

If you look back to the OCR text and the word coordinates for the first line from page three you'll see that the line 'All Men pretend the Licentiousness of the Press to be a publick Grievance' contains some errors: the OCR software has introduced stray punctuation marks and rendered 'All' as 'LL'. Despite the developing technology of OCR, it's only as useful as its accuracy in word recognition. In the case of ECCO, the accuracy and reliability of a user's search results depend entirely on the accuracy of the OCR engine to decipher eighteenth-century print.

More sophisticated text recognition can be achieved by an OCR engine that can match alternative spellings or find similar forms of a word (known as 'fuzzy' searching) – particularly important for printed texts published before the nineteenth century, which used a wide variety of spellings and word forms. The period of hand-press printing also produced idiosyncratic typography. For example, printers used the so-called long s (which superficially looks like an 'f'), ligatures (when two characters, for example, 'f' and 'l', are joined together as a single glyph on one single piece of type: fl), and the swash, or exaggerated serif. Also problematic are pages that combine text with images, tables, or diagrams. Such peculiarities are exacerbated by the huge variations in the quality of the material itself and the sheer human fallibility of handmade printing processes (such as skewed lines, ink bleed-through, under-inking leading to faded text, using worn or damaged metal type). All this means that OCR engines had and still have a real difficulty discerning the features of pre-1900 print.

If that were not enough, the fact that the OCR engine is reading a book that is twice remediated – first by filming, and second by

---

[35] The OCR software 'calculates a confidence level from 0 to 9 for each character it detects, but does not know whether a character has been converted correctly or not . . . True accuracy, that is, whether a character is actually correct, can only be determined by a human assessing each character manually'. Behind the Scenes at Gale – Creating a Digital Archive, www.gale.com/intl/archives-explored/behind-the-scenes/creating-a-digital-archive-technical [accessed 25 May 2020].

digitisation – introduces more barriers to the software's ability to render accurate text. Microfilming itself was not always an error-free process: witness JSTOR's decision to scan from the original paper documents and not from microfilms. Although quality control procedures were standard, a number of faults could be introduced at the filming stage, some of which could be rectified, and others not. These included spots or areas missing from faulty film, blurred images, missing pages, foreign objects showing, such as the operator's finger, inconsistent exposure resulting from changes in the density of the pages, and scratches on the film from grit in the camera (Ashby & Campbell, 1979: 81). A 1990 report by the University of California, Berkeley evaluated five US microform vendors, including RPI, and concluded that while most microfilming companies had basic acceptable standards, all had some minor faults, and RPI had a 'major fault' of missing pages (Lockhart & Swartzell, 1990: 120–3). Indeed, any full-text search of the 1789 issue of Browne's *The Civil and Natural History of Jamaica* will not find any words on the pages missing from its filming.

It is not surprising, then, that OCR is the most well-known topic in discussions of ECCO (Gadd, 2009; Greenfield, 2010; Spedding, 2011; Dane, 2012; Mandell, 2015; Hine, 2016; Prescott, 2018; Hill & Hengchen, 2019). For example, Ian Gadd revealed that 'the word "fuck" or versions thereof appear over 28,000 times,' revealing the OCR engine's tendency to misread the long 's' as an 'f'. It is unlikely that eighteenth-century printed material was much cruder in its language than we thought; in other words, the OCR engine has produced an alarming number of false positives (Gadd, 2009:10).[36] Moreover, while OCR software begins at the level of the character, a 2009 report on the OCR accuracy of the British Library's digitisation of newspapers remarked that the 'potential retrieval rate for a resource depends upon the OCR engine's accuracy with *significant words*, that is, those content words for which most users might be interested in searching, not the very common function words such as "the", "he", "it",

---

[36] If you try searching for the word 'suck' – a much more common printed word – the results are surprisingly low in comparison, suggesting that the completeness of these results is low (known as 'low recall').

etc.' (my emphasis).[37] The report found that the OCR accuracy with significant words was always *lower* than character or word accuracy rates, which 'may be due to such words being generally longer or not in dictionaries, which thus provides more statistical opportunity for error' (Tanner et al., 2009).[38] Optical character recognition accuracy can be calculated in different ways; later projects examined accuracy at the level of the page. For example, the Early Modern Optical Character Recognition Project (eMOP), which explored ways of improving OCR in both EEBO and ECCO, calculated ECCO's OCR 'correctness' at the level of the page as 86 per cent (Mandell, 2015: 2). However, the most recent and most systematic analysis revealed that its accuracy at the character level was very good, but at the page level it was noticeably lower at 77 per cent.[39] The analysis emphasised that 'OCR errors are not neutral' in ECCO since the peculiarities of eighteenth-century typography were a major factor in error and disproportionally affected long words, so perhaps the more significant words (Hill & Hengchen, 2019: 828, 840, 829–31).

To an extent, the precise figure for recognition accuracy is a distraction; the real issue is one of transparency. To be fair, Gale has always acknowledged that ECCO's OCR is fallible. On the original interface it was rather hidden in 'FAQs':

> There are some difficulties of applying optical character recognition technology to 18th century books, since the typefaces during this period contain many oddities such as the resemblance of s's to f's. However, in general, the OCR

---

[37] For some computer-aided analyses, particularly those that identify an author's style, these function words can be essential.

[38] As a point of comparison, the report's analysis of the digitised Burney Collection of eighteenth-century newspapers revealed accuracies of characters at 75.6 per cent, words at 65 per cent, and significant words at 48 per cent (Tanner et al., 2009). See also Prescott (2018).

[39] This is an average of two statistics: the completeness of the results, or the percentage of words which were recalled (81 per cent), and the precision or usefulness of the results (74 per cent).

> rates are in the low to mid 90%'s, with a fair amount of variation based on the type of font and language. Using fuzzy searching will help find additional matches for your search term, overcoming both incorrect OCR results as well as variant spellings.[40]

The note perhaps managed to both understate the problem and over-state the solution. Fuzzy searching might help to find additional matches, but it can't entirely overcome the challenges posed by the material and the processes by which it was initially filmed. Gale's initial decision to not make the underlying OCR text visible to users on the original interface was perhaps due to the fact that the OCR text 'contains enough errors to be distracting to the reader', as the TCP diplomatically put it.[41] In the chapter 'Interfacing', we'll see how Gale changed its stance towards the OCR text, but in this initial period the fact that the actual OCR text was not accessible in the original ECCO interface raised certain problems, particularly the necessary knowledge needed on the part of users. Increasingly scholars were using the large sets of textual data to conduct computer-aided quantitative analyses for posing questions about themes or topics, authorial style, or linguistic features, all of which depend, in essence, on counting words. But the accuracy of such counting crucially depends on knowing the quality of the textual data in order to know the limits and contexts of any results. A case in point was Peter de Bolla's fascinating study *The Architecture of Concepts: The Historical Formation of Human Rights* (2013). This used ECCO's interface to find keywords and the co-occurrence of other keywords to show how the concept of 'rights' shifted over the period. His note on methodology is interesting:

---

[40] Gale, ECCO, Research Tools: FAQs 'What Is the Accuracy Level of the OCR?' http://find.gale.com.bathspa.idm.oclc.org/ecco/researchTools [accessed 11 March 2020].

[41] Text Creation Partnership – Using TCP Content – Results of Keying, https://textcreationpartnership.org/using-tcp-content/results-of-keying/ [accessed 26 July 2020].

> As is now well known, the optical character recognition
> (OCR) software used by Gale, the publisher, compromises
> the reliability of the data extracted . . . But since I doubt that
> there will be significant changes to the profiles I have created
> for the concepts here studied, the revision of precise numer-
> ical values will be unlikely to lead to different conclusions.
> (de Bolla, 2013: 8)

Some responses to this study have pointed out de Bolla's overconfident
reliance on ECCO's online search capabilities, and the inconsistencies in his
note on methodology that acknowledges the fact that the OCR 'compro-
mises the reliability of the data', but at the same time is confident that this
will not compromise the conclusions (Baker, 2016; Prescott, 2018: 63–4).
The claim to the usefulness of the book's conclusions may be true: even
with 80 per cent accuracy, quantitative analyses can still produce mean-
ingful results (Hill & Hengchen, 2019: 840). However, without direct access
to the textual data, and without taking into account the exact nature of your
eighteenth-century data set, how does the researcher know what *wasn't*
found. In other words, you don't know what you don't know.

Searching the OCR text of the books in ECCO isn't the only way – and
perhaps not even the first way – users navigate the database. As I asked in
2007, 'Could students begin to use it as a research tool for themselves?'
(Gregg, 2007). Going by the second wave of responses to ECCO around
2007–9, in conference panel discussions and articles, academics and librarians assessed how they and their students reflected on the relationship
between access, discoverability, and searchability. Eighteenth Century
Collections Online arguably supported the turn towards historicisation
which emphasised the importance of contextual material in understanding
literary works; a related consequence was that courses could introduce texts
that pushed the boundaries of the canon, illuminating, for example,
neglected genres or writings by women (Aw, 2007; Gregg, 2007).
A special edition of *The Eighteenth-Century Intelligencer*, 'Teaching with
ECCO', explored how students could access texts held in libraries' special
collections and that are often inaccessible either financially or geographi-
cally; it also discussed how ECCO posed some initial challenges to students

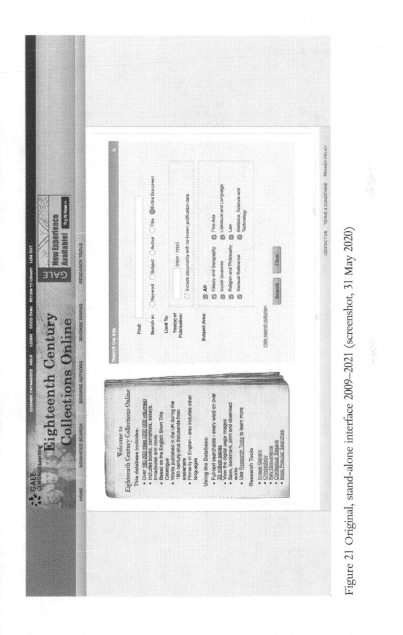

Figure 21 Original, stand-alone interface 2009–2021 (screenshot, 31 May 2020)

unfamiliar with database searching and the nature of such a large collection of historical material.

Given what Sayre Greenfield called this 'huge wilderness' of digitised primary material, how did ECCO's various search functions shape the way users navigated this wilderness or enable discovery (Greenfield, 2009: 13)? I want now to turn to how ECCO's original interface worked beneath its surface (Figure 21).

As Lori Emerson reminds us, 'interfaces themselves and therefore their constraints are becoming ever more difficult to perceive because of the blinding seduction of the wondrous': the interface itself is not a neutral or transparent window to the books in ECCO (Emerson, 2014: ix). Eighteenth Century Collections Online is not just what you see on the screen; it is a collection of files and systems that drive the capabilities of the interface: it shapes what the user is capable of doing with the books (which are themselves made up of image files, OCR text, and their associated bibliographical data). The search functions on ECCO's original interface were driven by a search engine based on Apache's Lucene. This might seem an arcane detail, but knowing that search software is an essential part of ECCO's workings also means that we might want to ask: when we search ECCO, what exactly is happening?

A 2003 prototype walk-through explained its search capabilities. From the 'Basic Search' box (later called 'Find', emphasising the aspect of discoverability) there were options to search four fields: the full text of the books, author, title, and keyword. We have already discussed the full-text search of the OCR'd text. Searches for author or title are enabled by the way in which the metadata for each book – essentially from the ESTC record – is structured in its XML file. In other words, the author or title search field searches for the author or title 'tag', as we can see from our example XML:

```
<authorGroup role="author">
<author>
<composed>Defoe, Daniel</composed>
<first>Daniel</first>
<last>Defoe</last>
<birthDate>1661?</birthDate>
```

```
<deathDate>1731</deathDate>
  </author>
  </authorGroup>
  <titleGroup>
<fullTitle>An essay on the regulation of the
press</fullTitle>
<displayTitle>An essay on the regulation of the
press</displayTitle>
  </titleGroup>
```

Users could, in addition, limit their search by defining 'Subject area'. This was always a confusing category, since it implied a notion of a book's 'subject', but this actually reflected the way in which the original microfilm collection was categorised and sold, and the subsequent publication of ECCO itself (such as 'Literature and Language', or 'Fine Arts', or 'History and Geography'). The process of adding metadata in ECCO also included tagging, which defined the following illustration types:

- Cartoon
- Chart
- Coat of Arms
- Genealogical Table
- Illustration
- Map
- Music
- Plan
- Portrait

This in turn enabled the facility in 'Advanced search' to limit searches by specific types of illustration.

However, how do we know what we're looking for before we discover it? The ability to discover new and unfamiliar texts using ECCO's 'keyword' search function was felt to be one of its most powerful capabilities to enable a kind of serendipitous navigation of this huge database (Greenfield, 2009). In this option the search engine's algorithm was actually searching across multiple fields:

- Author (including any secondary author fields)
- Title (and all variations of the title – short title, full title, variant title, etc.)
- Chapter headings, which is essentially equivalent to the info that you see in the e-TOC (minus the three major headings: Front Matter, Main Body, Back Matter)
- Library of Congress subject headings (when available in mid-2008)[42]

The chapter and section headings were scanned as part of the digitisation and were used to create an 'e-Table of Contents' (e-TOC) in order to enable navigation within each text, but were also tagged in the XML file so they would be searchable. The last field mentioned in the keyword search, 'Library of Congress subject headings', refers to the original interface's search capabilities from 2008 onwards. From this date the interface offered one more additional field to its Basic Search or Find box: 'Subject'.

This wasn't the same as Gale's subject areas, but it was a library subject heading, and it vastly enhanced the usefulness of ECCO's keyword searching. The Library of Congress maintains the classification system for subject headings that is the standard for library cataloguing around the world.[43] Subject headings are a form of bibliographic metadata that attempts to categorise a book's intellectual content, rather than details about its physical form. For example, the subject headings for Patrick Browne, *The Civil and Natural History of Jamaica* (1789) are:

Tropical medicine – Early works to 1800
Medical climatology – Early works to 1800
Natural history – Jamaica – Early works to 1800

Subject headings offer the user the ability to discover material based on what might initially be a mere hunch, without any necessary knowledge as to titles or authors of the material. It was this added value that researchers

---

[42] Gale, ECCO, Research Tools: FAQs 'What Does a Keyword Search Cover?', http://find.gale.com.bathspa.idm.oclc.org/ecco/researchTools [accessed 11 March 2020].

[43] Library of Congress Subject Headings, http://id.loc.gov/authorities/subjects .html [accessed 20 April 2020].

conducting a Northwestern University library experiment in 2005 sought to test in relation to the material in ECCO. In order to do this they gathered a sample of around 52,000 records from WorldCat, in which they found 'a total of 30,948 different subject headings were applied 107,477 times – an average of slightly more than two subject headings per title'; these headings were then imported to their local catalogue records for ECCO (Garrett, 2007: 71). The project tested the effectiveness of subject headings by pitting searches in the subject heading field against searches conducted just by title or just in the full text. In both cases the project found that searches using subject headings found significantly more texts than either title or full-text searches (Garrett, 2007: 73–5). For example, a title may not contain the phrase you're looking for, even though the book might; however, this does not necessarily mean that the full text of the book contains this phrase either: in the example just given, a search for 'climatology' would return no results at all since the term didn't exist in the period. As Jeffrey Garrett puts it, subject headings are a 'Meta-vocabulary' and their utility in a full-text database like ECCO is how they enable 'searching and discovery, across centuries and across languages' (Garrett, 2007: 75).

As we've seen, the search engine in keyword mode searches a number of metadata fields including the subject headings. But I want to dig a little deeper in order to differentiate this type of data from other ECCO fields, since this is not a purely machine-driven process: unlike the OCR text, or the title or author, the subject heading was assigned by a combination of human interpretation and computer-aided harvesting of data. Between 2005 and 2007 the Center for Bibliographic Studies and Research at the University of California, Riverside – the headquarters of the ESTC – began a project to update its subject headings. This was largely due to the fact that while records for material before 1700 incorporated subject headings, material after that date did not – in other words, the books catalogued by the 18thC STC and eventually digitised in ECCO (Garrett, 2007: 70). Part of this project involved the Northwestern University experiment in 2005, but the ESTC also tasked HTC Global in 2007 to add subject headings to the ESTC's catalogue records, starting with around 63,000 ECCO titles. In this project HTC operators examined the existing ESTC records, used the digitised images to read portions of the works, and finally assigned subject headings to each work using the Library of Congress subject headings list (Geiger & Schilling, 2016). Eighteenth Century Collections Online's enhancement of its metadata and the MARC library records it sells in addition to the database was completed around 2009. In 2012 the interface's 'FAQs' described how '[o]ver 274,000 subject headings' were added 'through the combination of harvesting and manual assignment'. Some subject headings were obtained from 'existing' library records which held the physical copy, and where this was not possible, 'ESTC licensed the work of adding LoC headings' (in other words, the HTC Global project).[44]

This suggests considerable potential for divergence between these two systems of gathering and assigning subject headings, driven as they were by different organisations and groups of people. In short, the subject headings can be idiosyncratic. I am reminded of a search I conducted when I wanted to find out what other works of fiction were published in the same year as Samuel Richardson's *Clarissa* (1748) – a book I was teaching at the time. Using 'Fiction' and 'English fiction' as subject heading terms in ECCO I found twenty-two titles. However, the same search in the ESTC produced a different set of results. This rough-and-ready exercise set me on a different path and made me think about how these databases categorise print history (Gregg, 2016). There are disparities in the bibliographical metadata between the ESTC and ECCO (May, 2009). But a few brief examples concerning the subject headings reveal much about the odd processes behind the creation and management of metadata in ECCO. Whoever tagged Ovid's *Heroides. English Ovid's epistles . . . Translated into English verse* as 'fiction' clearly didn't understand the title. And why wasn't Henry Fielding's canonical novel *The History of the Adventures of Joseph Andrews* tagged as 'fiction' in ECCO? It wasn't a case of looking at the title and thinking, 'well, this is a history or a biography'. Both the ESTC and ECCO give this the specific subject heading 'Tobacco-fiction', a peculiarly specific heading assigned to just three titles in the entire ESTC; the other two are novels by Tobias Smollett: *The Adventures of Peregrine Pickle*

---

[44] Eighteenth Century Collections Online, Part I and Part II FAQs – Gale, 2012, https://web.archive.org/web/20120331004819/ http://gdc.gale.com/pro ducts/eighteenth-century-collections-online/acquire/faqs/#partii-loc [accessed 21 July 2020].

(1751) and *The Expedition of Humphry Clinker* (1773). Now, it's true that people smoke in these novels, but plenty of other protagonists from the fiction of the period smoke. Such idiosyncrasies are illuminating because the creation of this metadata reveals the tangled history of the 18thC STC, the ESTC, and ECCO, and the peculiar mix of machines and human agency that underpins the search interface.

Nevertheless, by 2009 Gale's upgrades to ECCO were considerable. Not only had it added the subject field to its metadata, it had upgraded its OCR to ABBYY, and it had published ECCO phase II of another 46,000 titles. In addition, Gale was listening to its library users and scholars: from 2007 the ECCO interface included a cross-search facility with EEBO so that, if the library had access to both databases, users could conduct searches within the ECCO interface to access the pre-1700 material digitised in EEBO (Rogers, 2007). Another example was the issue of ESTC metadata. Scholars such as Eleanor Shevlin were discussing how databases like ECCO might enable a more interactive relationship to ESTC data and 'provide opportunities to correct bibliographical inaccuracies' (in Battigelli, 2010). From 2012 ECCO's 'Full Citation' window included an email link entitled 'Report an issue with this ECCO/ESTC record'.

It should also be clear that ECCO has never been a static entity. Scholars using ECCO clearly influenced the upgrades to the original interface in these years. But the design of ECCO was forcefully shaped by the landscape of academic electronic publishing in the mid- to late 1990s. Gale perceived a gap in existing academic and educational digital resources and capitalised on its existing content: the microfilm collection The Eighteenth Century. To a significant extent, this constrained ECCO's capabilities in terms of how the books looked and the effectiveness of full-text searching. Nevertheless, Gale deployed state-of-the-art digitisation and data handling technologies in order to push to the limits what could be achieved with microfilm. The sum of these decisions shaped how ECCO could be searched, how these books could be discovered, and how we users apprehend eighteenth-century books. The next chapter explores how concerns about the usability of the underlying OCR text, as well as the costs of access, led to a number of licensing deals and collaborative projects that – together with Gale's own developments – offered new ways of using, accessing, and interfacing with ECCO.

5 Interfacing

As of May 2020, when I'm writing this, there are in fact a number of different ways of accessing or interfacing with ECCO. From Gale there is the original 'stand-alone' interface (now called a 'legacy' interface, scheduled to be switched off by 2021) and the two cross-database platforms Gale Primary Sources and Gale Digital Scholar Lab. However, since the launch of ECCO in 2003 it has become part of a wider digital conglomerate of licensing deals and partnerships. This includes a print-on-demand arrangement with BiblioLife, the TCP which edited and published more than 2,000 ECCO texts, and the US-based platform 18thConnect. Finally, Jisc enables UK-only access to the full range of ECCO images and text via its platform Historical Texts. But the effect of these on what 'access' means will curiously echo our earlier discussion of access in relation to the praise of microfilm by such as Robert Binkley and H. G. Wells.

Partnerships, Licensing, and Access, 2004–2020

The interface is not a transparent portal to access, as Tim Sherratt has argued. 'Online interfaces make assumptions about the needs and desires of users. They do not merely provide access; they construct it by defining the types of interactions we can have with collections' (Sherratt, 2019: 4). The issue of ECCO's OCR overlapped with a wider discussion about what 'access' meant in relation to how digital texts might be used and transformed outside the confines of commercial interfaces. At the same time, academics and libraries were also expressing concerns about the cost of accessing ECCO and what was becoming known as a 'digital divide' in higher education institutions. In effect, this continues our exploration of the cultural and technological issues surrounding the questions of how we access old books that started with our discussion of Robert Binkley and Eugene Power's hopes for microfilm in the 1930s.

Eighteenth Century Collections Online's first partnership was with the TCP. The TCP was directly responding to the question of how access to digital texts could be enhanced and transformed. It aimed to enable its partners of libraries and commercial publishers to

- pool their resources in order to create full-text resources few could afford individually
- create texts to a common standard suitable for search, display, navigation, and reuse
- collaborate with commercial providers, rather than constantly bargaining and competing with them.[45]

As we've seen, the project initially aimed to give users the ability to conduct full-text searches of the material in EEBO. Given the limitations of OCR software working on hand-press printed material, the texts selected by the TCP were transcribed by hand, and were to be 'transcribed by more than one person, and the results are compared against one another, to generate electronic text that is 99.95 per cent accurate'.[46] By 2019 EEBO-TCP had transcribed around 40,000 texts.[47] The ECCO-TCP project began in 2004. However, it turned out to be on a much smaller scale than the EEBO-TCP project. This was arguably because its aims were less coherent than for EEBO-TCP, given that a searchable text was already available via ECCO. Transcriptions continued until 2011, although a requested selection of medical texts was transcribed in 2012 (Schaffner, 2019). The ECCO-TCP project was expected to transcribe around 10,000 texts, but only 2,473 texts were eventually created (Blaney, 2019).[48] The texts were released to Gale in several batches between 2005 and 2012; in 2011, by agreement with Gale, 2,231 texts were released to the public, and were also searchable via 18thConnect (Mandell, 2011;

---

[45] Text Creation Partnership, https://textcreationpartnership.org/ [accessed 4 January 2020].

[46] Text Creation Partnership – Results of Keying, https://textcreationpartnership .org/using-tcp-content/results-of-keying/ [accessed 4 January 2020].

[47] Text Creation Partnership – EEBO-TCP, https://textcreationpartnership.org/ tcp-texts/eebo-tcp-early-english-books-online/# [accessed 4 January 2020].

[48] The final figure does not include around 628 texts that were not subject to final proofing or editing. Text Creation Partnership – ECCO-TCP, https://text creationpartnership.org/tcp-texts/ecco-tcp-eighteenth-century-collections-online/ [accessed 4 January 2020].

Schaffner, 2019).[49] They were made available via Jisc's Historical Texts platform in 2016.[50] These were small numbers compared with EEBO-TCP. Funding was the problem: as early as 2006 the executive board was proposing ways to ensure future funding in order to ameliorate predicted budget deficits.[51] As the director of the TCP, Paul Schaffner, recalls, 'we never received the financial support that we hoped for', so the period between 2009 and the final transcription in 2012 saw the project gradually wind down (Schaffner, 2019). Shawn Martin (the TCP project librarian at Michigan and an executive board member) pointed out that while 'one could argue that because of OCR text running behind the images in . . . ECCO, a TCP project is not needed, it is also true that many kinds of research need the added value that TCP offers to encourage electronic scholarship' (Martin, 2009: 6). The 2,000-plus texts of ECCO-TCP are publicly available and are free to use, analyse, edit, modify, and even republish without copyright restrictions, and can be accessed via a number of digital archives and spin-off projects (Gregg, 2019). The ECCO-TCP project provided the 'ground truth' for the eMOP project to test the accuracy of its OCR engine's performance against the hand-transcribed texts of the TCP (Mandell, 2015: Appendix C). The TCP set also plays a part in a variety of archives and large-scale text analyses, such as the Eighteenth-Century Poetry Archive (2012), Visualizing English Print (2015 ongoing), Linguistic DNA (2015 ongoing), and Commonplace Cultures (2016 ongoing).

One of the TCP's aims was to create access to texts 'few could afford'. The crucial context in the late twentieth century that was shaping the debates about online access to scholarship was the drive towards 'open

---

[49] The different numbers reflect the fact that transcription continued after the 2011 public release: texts transcribed after 2011 were not subject to any public access embargo.

[50] Jisc Historical Texts – Development Roadmap, https://historicaltexts.Jisc.ac .uk/developmentroadmap [accessed 27 July 2020].

[51] TCP Executive Board Meeting Minutes, 16 September 2006, https://wayback .archive-it.org/5871/20190806191843/ http://www.textcreationpartnership .org/tcp-board-meeting-minutes-2006-09-16/ [accessed 25 August 2020].

access'. As Kathleen Fitzpatrick summarised it, this is the 'ethical desire to break down the barrier between the information "haves" and "have nots" of the twenty-first-century university structure' (Fitzpatrick, 2011: 160). The notion of universal access to knowledge had been present since the early twentieth century, with thinkers and scholars such as Robert Binkley and H. G. Wells' notions in his book *World Brain* (1938), but the advent of the World Wide Web and large digitisation projects accelerated the means and intensified the stakes of what 'access' meant. Martin Paul Eve identifies two socio-historical drivers: the 'serials crisis' in academic publishing and libraries, and the 'free culture' ethos (Eve, 2014: 12–21). What Eve terms the 'serials crisis' was the symptom of both an exponential increase in scholarly research in the last half of the twentieth century and an increase in publishers' pricing of journal subscriptions that outstripped inflation and library budgets, resulting in 'paywalls that hinder [the] ability to conduct research and to teach/learn efficiently' (Eve, 2014: 13). Simultaneously, late twentieth-century commercialised information technology gave rise to a 'counter-discourse of "free culture"' which was articulated not solely in terms of cost, but more as the 'freedom to reuse material' (17). This addressed, in other words, the difficult relationship between the holder of the copyright to a work and the user's ability – or not – to reuse that material. The two concerns about scholarly publishing and free culture eventually came together in a series of defining documents in 2002 and 2003 (21). We'll see how this democratising impulse fed through to ECCO's licensing deals and partnerships.

The debates around digitisation and access to knowledge were to become particularly febrile following the legal challenges to the mass digitisation of millions of books by Google Books. Its explosive programme of scanning in the early 2000s broached the border between out-of-copyright works and works still under copyright: its vision of universal access came forcefully up against the commercial interests of publishers and the rights of authors, resulting in a complex series of legal challenges and appeals by the Authors Guild of America (working with the Association of American Publishers) and Google between 2005 and 2014. In 2008, at the height of these proceedings, Google proposed to award a $125 million settlement in return for considerable rights to the material it had digitised.

However, scholars, librarians, and internet activists were concerned that Google, far from freeing the world's knowledge, was effectively monopolising it (Darnton, 2012; Somers, 2017; Thylstrup, 2018: 45–8).[52]

These arguments were echoed in 2015, albeit briefly, between scholars and the publisher of EEBO, ProQuest. Unusually, since EEBO was a library-only subscription, the very large membership of the Renaissance Society of America had been granted access; however, in October 2015 ProQuest cancelled that subscription because, as the society surmised, its members' 'heavy use' threatened ProQuest's 'potential revenue from library-based subscriptions' (cited in Wexler, 2015). The reaction from the society's membership was immediate, as users took to Twitter to complain with the hashtags #EEBOgate, #ProQuestGate, and #FrEEBO. ProQuest quickly reversed its decision, but users were outraged by how easily commercial publishers could bar access to research. John Overholt thought this should be a 'wakeup call . . . These books are part of our cultural heritage, and it's high time we made them available to *everyone*' (Overholt, 2015). #EEBOgate certainly gained traction coming so soon after the collapse of the case against Google Books in 2014.

This discourse about paywalls and free culture was also heard in earlier questions about Gale's ECCO. Certainly, it's a fact that ECCO's price point kept it out of the smaller colleges and universities. 'Access doesn't come cheap', one reviewer commented at its launch, while another noted that its 'price tag may be a hurdle for many libraries' (Smith, 2003; Levack, 2003). In December 2009 Peter Reill (then president of the American Society for Eighteenth-Century Studies), sent a message via the email discussion group C-18 L to address 'the question of the increasingly unequal access of scholars to digital resource databases that are critical to pursuing research in their fields', and set out a number of questions for the society to debate:

> How important is access to commercial databases to scholars
> in your field, and how are scholars' careers affected when
> they are at institutions that do not subscribe to those

---

[52] The final judgment of 2014 ruled in favour of Google, but left the status of Google's digitisation of books in legal uncertainty.

resources? Which databases are likely to be of greatest value to the broadest segment of your membership? How well situated is your society to serve as a conduit to these resources, and what would be required to make that possible? (Reill, 2009)

The issue of affordability for libraries mentioned in some of the first reviews of ECCO had by 2009 been transformed into the issue of 'unequal access'. The issue was picked up by the *Early Modern Online Bibliography* blog, which generated a number of comments; in one, Anna Battigelli argued that:

> The digital divide enforced by the question of access further encourages administrators to view their institutions as deficient in the archives needed for these earlier [period] positions. Recruiting and retention of faculty becomes more challenging. The case for eliminating pre-1800 positions becomes more attractive. As smaller institutions decide against recruiting eighteenth-century scholars, fewer graduate students at larger institutions will venture into the field.

As Battigelli draws out the interdependency of library resources, staffing, and student recruitment, she ends with the striking conclusion: 'The health of eighteenth-century studies – or of any form of early modern studies – is at stake' (in Shevlin, 2009).

One unique response to the digital divide was Ben Pauley's 'Eighteenth-Century Book Tracker', an online archive created as a solution to the lack of access at his own college. As Pauley describes it, this was intended to be 'a clearinghouse for registering links to freely-available digital facsimiles of eighteenth-century texts, pooling its users' discoveries and attaching them to bibliographically responsible entries' (Pauley, 2009). Book Tracker was an attempt to offer an alternative to Gale's pay-walled ECCO by collating and indexing links to eighteenth-century books digitised elsewhere (largely, Google Books) and contributed by a scholarly community of users. However, from 2019 the site lost its crowdsourcing functionality: it was, as its creator acknowledged, a one-person operation and difficult to sustain.[53] Pauley's project brings to the fore the tension within the wider debate about open access: the long-held idealism of universal knowledge and the economic realities required to enable and sustain such ideals.

There is actually a non-digital way of accessing ECCO titles. From 2010 BiblioLife began producing print-on-demand (POD) copies of Gale's digital collections under the licensed 'ECCO Print Editions' imprint. This comprised around 117,000 titles; as with ECCO, Gale pays royalties to the source library for every copy sold (Dawson, in Shevlin 2010). In POD publishing the electronic files are held by the publisher and copies are printed and bound only when a customer, via an online retailer such as Amazon, orders a copy. Print-on-demand publishing owed much to the availability of digital printers in the 1990s that could print off small numbers at low unit cost, and was initially used to print technical instruction manuals (Thompson, 2005: 421–2). Later the giant Ingram publishing company saw the possibilities for revolutionising the business of publishing books; as one source put it, 'It used to be print book, sell book. We say, no, no. Sell book, print book' (quoted in Thompson, 2005: 422).

Indeed, BiblioLife does not define itself as a publisher: 'We are really a software company that has books coming out at the end of our process' (quoted in Albanese, 2010). BiblioLife is based in Charleston, South Carolina, and is the umbrella company to a number of POD subsidiaries including BiblioBazaar and Nabu Press, and it is owned by BiblioLabs LLC (Wikipedia Contributors, 2019). BiblioLife specialises in publishing historical reprints, and its president defined its business model as 'really focused on unique materials that are not part of mass digitization projects . . . Who has that content and how we are getting it is something that is a competitive advantage' (quoted in Albanese, 2010). However, this pugnacious self-image of BiblioLife is slightly contradicted by its more utopian blurb inside the covers of ECCO Print Editions. In this POD copy of a 1704 pamphlet by Daniel Defoe BiblioLife explains its part in a project called the BiblioLife Network:

[53] Eighteenth-Century Book Tracker – About, http://benjaminpauley.net/c18booktracker/about [accessed 21 January 2020].

We believe every book ever published should be available as a high-quality print reproduction; printed on-demand anywhere in the world. This insures [*sic*] the ongoing accessibility of the content and helps generate sustainable revenue for the libraries and organizations that work to preserve these important materials. (Defoe, 2010)

Rather than leveraging a niche marketing opportunity, BiblioLife's mission is ostensibly part of a long-standing ethos to preserve and provide access to important historical heritage – which is perhaps beside the point, because in one way, by making available low-demand historical materials at low cost (relative to institutional digital access costs), there is an echo of Binkley's and Power's hopes for accessing old books I explored earlier in relation to microfilm.

BiblioLife's branding – 'old books, new life' – might alert us to consider what kind of 'life' this is. The reaction to some POD copies of old books homed in on their peculiar lack of bookishness: many do not include information about how they are produced, or what edition or source copy has been used (Shevlin, 2010). It is for this reason Whitney Trettien termed these books 'zombie-like', as if their previous life has been cut away (Trettien, 2013). However, BiblioLife's ECCO Print Editions are unusually forthcoming on metadata and the processes of remediation. ECCO's metadata and ESTC numbers are reproduced in Amazon's product description and in the inside cover of each POD book 'in the interest of increasing the chance of edition identification' (Scott Dawson, in Shevlin, 2010).

Gale's own inside cover blurb also emphasises the ability to access its digitised books outside the paywall of a subscription database: 'Now for the first time, these high-quality digital scans of original works are available via print-on-demand, making them readily accessible to libraries, students, independent scholars, and readers of all ages' (Defoe, 2010). The argument was echoed by scholars and couched in terms of widening access: 'One thing that is great about ECCO's POD service through BiblioLife is that those without access to ECCO can get access to selected works, admittedly at a price. This may not be the perfect solution to access problems, but it is a bit better than having no access at all' (Battigelli, in Shevlin, 2010).

Other scholars and institutions were collaborating with Gale to ameliorate the digital divide and to widen access. One is the US-based academic community platform 18thConnect. This was linked to eMOP, the OCR project already mentioned, and was initially conceived in 2009 at a digital humanities meeting in Dublin.[54] 18thConnect acts as an open-access searchable aggregator platform for a large number of eighteenth-century resources, including ECCO. Users find results in ECCO but still need institutional access to click through to the images in the collection. Its founder, Laura Mandell, had also wanted to create a tool to correct ECCO's OCR. In 2010 Gale granted 18thConnect 'a limited, nonexclusive, royalty-free right to use the Typed Plain Text, OCR Plain Text and Metadata' (Mandell: 2012b: 23). In July 2010 the National Endowment for the Humanities granted an award of $41,000 for '18thConnect: an open access resource', out of which 'Typewright', a crowdsourcing correction tool, was developed (Mandell, 2019a). The Typewright interface sits on the 18thConnect website and enables users to pull up the raw OCR text from ECCO underneath a window which shows a snippet view from the corresponding page image; users then manually correct the OCR text. However, once a complete text has been corrected, 18thConnect sends the user/editor the full corrected text *'to use as he or she likes'*, but principally with the hope of creating scholarly editions, echoing the aims of open access and scholarly reuse exemplified in the TCP project (Mandell, 2012a: 302; emphasis in the original).[55]

The most significant alternative access to ECCO – for the United Kingdom – is Jisc's platform, Historical Texts. The Joint Information Systems Committee (Jisc) was formed in 1993 in order to manage and develop UK network and information systems for an ever-expanding

---

[54] Advanced Research Consortium – History, http://ar-c.org/about/history-2/ [accessed 2 January 2020].

[55] The aim was that corrected OCR text would be sent to Gale to be incorporated into ECCO. However, as of late 2019, no texts had been sent, partly because the number of corrected texts was small (270) and partly because Gale was worried it would have to adjust the word coordinates (Mandell, 2019a, 2019b).

higher education system.[56] After the 1993 Follet report on university libraries, Jisc was allocated £15 million to create and oversee various projects that would enhance its digital capabilities, called the 'Electronic Libraries Programme' ('eLib').[57] Jisc began to function as national negotiator enabling access to licensed content on behalf of the UK education community, which enabled Jisc to achieve significant cost benefits. Notably, Jisc also enables UK Further Education institutes, with students aged between sixteen and eighteen, to access digital resources.

Jisc Collections' major coup was signing licensing agreements with ProQuest for EEBO, and with Gale for ECCO I in 2006 and for ECCO II in 2009.[58] These would form the basis for Jisc's Historic Books platform, which began development in 2011, and was redesigned in 2014 as Historical Texts. The platform now offers access to 'over 460,000 late 15th to 19th century texts', including the British Library's 19thC Collection and non-paywalled access to the UK Medical Heritage Library, and there are plans to add access to the Burney Collection of eighteenth-century newspapers.[59] The deal included page image files and the XML files for the OCR text plus bibliographical metadata; they were bought from Gale in perpetuity, while Gale retained the copyright for the images (Gibbens, 2019). When it came to the MARC library records for the material (these enable each individual record to be loaded on to a library's catalogue) Jisc bypassed the necessity for buying MARC records from Gale by securing a partnership deal directly with the ESTC and then added its own enhancements, thereby securing a better deal for UK higher education institutions. In addition, Historic

---

[56] Jisc – About – History, www.Jisc.ac.uk/about/history# [accessed 20 February 2020].

[57] e-Lib: The Electronic Libraries Programme 1995–2001, www.ukoln.ac.uk/services/elib/ [accessed 28 July 2020].

[58] Digital Humanities @ Oxford – Project – Eighteenth Century Collections Online, https://digital.humanities.ox.ac.uk/project/eighteenth-century-collections-online-ecco [accessed 27 July 2020].

[59] Historical Texts, https://historicaltexts.Jisc.ac.uk; Historical Texts – Development Roadmap, https://historicaltexts.Jisc.ac.uk/developmentroadmap [accessed 27 July 2020].

Texts was able to ingest the ECCO-TCP set (the ECCO texts transcribed by the TCP), since Jisc had been a member of the partnership (Marchionni & Milloy, 2020).

Historical Texts is part of the 'Jisc eCollections' programme' launched in 2011. As Caren Milloy (the director of licensing since 2020) described it, this is 'a community-owned content service developed to protect and preserve existing content investments by offering an alternative to commercial providers. It brings access fees within the control of the community, in terms of ring-fenced reinvestment and moderation of increases' (Milloy, 2012). A particular source of frustration in UK libraries is the pricing structure of digital collections. Jisc's reports 'Digital Archive Collections Platform Charging Survey' (2018) and 'Library Collections: Navigating the Payment for Access Minefield' (Findlay, 2019) highlight how, on top of the one-off perpetual cost, additional costs are associated with yearly 'hosting' or 'platform' fees, and there is also the cost of hard drives publishers sell in order to enable users to conduct text analysis (known as 'TDM' drives). Gale's TDM drives, which contain OCR text and metadata, cost between $500 and $1000 per resource, more if it is a particularly large collection (Gale, 2014). On hosting or platform fees, one report found that in the 'last academic year' 46 per cent of respondents spent up to £5,000, while 33 per cent spent more than £15,000 on these fees (Jisc, 2018, in Findlay, 2019).

It is tempting to see Jisc's Historical Texts as a competitor of Gale's ECCO in the United Kingdom, but this is to ask the wrong question. In an interview with Paola Marchionni (the head of digital resources for teaching, learning, and research) she acknowledged that Jisc wants to provide a 'better deal' for the UK education community and to recoup costs. However, she insisted that 'we don't see ourselves as publishers … the drivers are different.' Marchionni contrasted the effectiveness of Jisc to enable access to digital content in the United Kingdom with the bigger digital 'divide' in academic institutions in the United States and Australia, and she was emphatic that Jisc's aim is to 'democratise access across the sector' (Marchionni & Milloy, 2020).

Academics were aware of the economics of sustaining digitisation, but there were tensions in attitudes. Laura Mandell recalled her initial outrage at the commercialisation of public heritage, but while developing the eMOP project at Texas University, she acknowledged that collaborative projects between libraries, academics, and commercial publishers like Gale are capable of effectively sustaining scholarly resources (Mandell, 2015: 2–3). In relation to the 18thConnect platform, Mandell noted her 'thanks to Gale for its openness to scholarly needs'.[60] However, community, openness, and commercial profit are difficult philosophies to reconcile. More recently, Gale's presence at conferences, both as keynote speaker and as sponsor of those conferences, has caused some concern. During my own talk about ECCO at the Digital Humanities Congress in Sheffield in 2018, I was bemused at my position: accepting a glass of Gale's sponsored wine just after having offered a critique of ECCO. Concerns were more seriously voiced during the large annual international digital humanities conference organised by the Alliance of Digital Humanities Organisations in Krakow in 2016. Conference goers took to Twitter to express their discomfort: for many the issue was that Gale's presentation – about its TDM drives – sounded more like a promotion of its product and so directly opposed the spirit of scholarship. In a follow-up piece, 'What Price Gale Cengage?', Andrew Prescott summarised these tensions nicely: while acknowledging that sponsorship is valuable for the running of large conferences, he noted that the 'production by Gale of enormously expensive digital packages which can only be afforded by university libraries seems at odds with the open access aspirations of many digital humanities practitioners'. The desire that 'contents of libraries, archives and museums owned by the public and part of a shared cultural heritage' should not be behind an expensive paywall reflected the aspirations of those who viewed with dismay #EEBOgate and the Google settlement discussions (Prescott, 2016).

Platforms

On one hand, Gale's genuine wish to engage with its users echoes the early aims Macomber voiced when ECCO was launched in 2003 (Hane, 2004). On the other hand, Gale is a commercial entity that has to sustain its proprietary investments and to recoup costs through development and sales. Eighteenth Century Collections Online's development in the 2010s was influenced by the

---

[60] 18thConnect – News, www.18thconnect.org/news/?p=49 [accessed 5 November 2019].

techno-commercial move towards platforms and apps, and also by its increasing awareness of digital humanities scholarship and practice, and in particular the use of computer-aided text analysis. Its response leveraged the idea of an enhanced interface that would enable users to directly work with text from across a diverse range of its products, resulting in the Gale Primary Sources and Gale Digital Scholar Lab platforms, launched in 2016 and 2019, respectively. Accessing ECCO via either Gale Primary Sources or Gale's Lab, or even Jisc's Historical Texts, is a fundamental shift away from the conception of an interface as the identifying face of a particular online collection. In 2020 Gale staff called the original ECCO interface the 'legacy' and 'stand-alone' interface, terms that together suggest that, as an interface designed solely for the digitisation of as single collection, it is outdated and it is time for it to be superseded (Sullivan, 2020). As I write, ProQuest is also scheduled to retire its stand-alone interface for EEBO and replace it with the 'ProQuest Platform'.[61] Welcome to the age of the platform.

The 'rise of the platform' – or 'platformisation' – has been associated with the big social media products such as Facebook, Twitter, and YouTube, but also with mass digitisation projects such as Google's, and even with how libraries can be conceptualised (Weinberger, 2012; Mattern, 2014; Helmond, 2015; Thylstrup, 2018: 126–31). But this use is itself built on older meanings. Tarleton Gillespie, developing the definitions offered by the OED, identified 'four semantic territories that the word "platform" has signified in the past' (Gillespie, 2010: 349). The first of these meanings is *computational*: 'an infrastructure that supports the design and use of particular applications' such as operating systems, hardware, or online applications and tools (Gillespie, 2010: 349). Gale uses the term in this sense to describe its internal digital infrastructure. Eighteenth Century Collections Online is separate from its interfaces, and is a collection amongst many within Gale's internal platforms. For instance, the original stand-alone interface for ECCO is underpinned by a backend platform linked to a search engine it shares with other collections (such as British Library Newspapers and the Burney

---

[61] ProQuest Early English Books Online on the ProQuest Platform, https://proquest.libguides.com/eebopqp [accessed 31 May 2020].

Collection). These collections are scheduled in 2020–1 to be migrated to a new backend platform driven by a content repository and an updated and highly modified version of the Lucene search engine which, in turn, underpins the Gale Primary Sources and Gale Digital Scholar Lab platforms (Sullivan, 2020).

This is of critical consequence for search results: they will be different depending on which interface or platform you are using (or have used). For simplicity's sake we can test this using the singe-box 'basic search' function and try the word 'dog'. This produced the following hits:

- Original, stand-alone interface: 52,449
- Gale Primary Sources: 73,686
- Gale Digital Scholar Lab: 73,686
- Historical Texts: 58,848

The last set of results illuminates what Kelly Centrelli noted in an early review of Jisc's Historic Books (the first version of Historical Texts): that the same search in ECCO and in Historic Books produced 'completely different' results because of its 'contextual word' searches (Centrelli, 2012). The results are produced by the configuration of Jisc's own backend platform, its own search engine, and a particular search algorithm: the history of this particular platform also reveals a history of changing backend systems.[62] In short, search results are shaped by the search algorithms peculiar to each interface.

Each of Gale's interfaces uses a customised search algorithm, or what Gale terms a 'search recipe'. I will exemplify how such an algorithm works for the 'basic search' function in Gale's Lab in order to explore how its search recipe builds and sorts results according to 'relevance'. The search recipe 'specifies which indexes to search and the proximity operators to apply. This determines how many articles are retrieved, and what the

---

[62] Jisc's first version, Historic Books (2011–13), was developed with the Autonomy search software company. After a wholesale redesign it was relaunched as Historical Texts in 2014 with an interface designed by Knowledge Integration, and using the ElasticSearch software (Gibbens, 2019).

relevance score of each of those articles will be' (Sullivan, 2020). The 'basic search' recipe looks like this:

```
{stemming=true;subjectExpansion=true;
fields=TI|SU|KE|TXT;operator=N4} (Houghton,
2020)
```

'Stemming' tells the search engine to search for different word endings; for example, if you searched 'dog', it would also find 'dogs' ('true' and 'false' are Boolean-like values that equate to yes/no or on/off).[63] 'Subject expansion' is a feature which uses machine-aided indexing: the search engine finds the word in the 'subject' field but then goes to Gale's local thesaurus, a master index of linked subject terms, in order to find other terms related to the original search word and then to search for them too. For example, 'dog' might also bring up results for 'canine'. The reason the ECCO standalone interface returns fewer hits for 'dog' is that its search engine's algorithm does *not* include the subject expansion option. The search recipe also defines which fields are to be included in the search; in this case title (TI), subject (SU), keyword (KE), and all the OCR'd text of the document (TXT). The KE (or keyword index) searches the first fifty words in a document as well as the author and table of contents fields. Finally, if the user puts two or more words into the search field the 'operator' function defines the proximity within which the search engine will find these words; in this case, each word has to be within four words (N4) of each other. After the search engine has processed each part of the recipe, it sorts the results in terms of 'relevance'. Essentially, each part of the recipe is weighted by points: the more parts of the recipe the search term is found within, the more points it scores, and the higher up the 'relevance' list it will appear.

Gillespie outlines other meanings of the platform; the oldest of which is *architectural*, as in a physical structure upon which people or things stand. The further, figurative meaning extends this sense of an architecture as a metaphor 'for opportunity, action and insight' (Gillespie, 2010: 350). Jisc's Historical Texts echoes the architectural sense of the term,

---

[63] Stemming, however, itself requires an algorithm that attempts to account for the idiosyncrasies of language itself.

describing itself as a 'platform' that 'brings together four historically significant collections for the first time'.[64] Other digital collections mobilise both figurative and computational meanings. The Digital Public Library of America (DPLA), for example, launched itself as both a 'portal' and a 'platform'; exploring the DPLA, but also digital libraries such as Europeana and Trove, Tim Sherratt usefully articulates the difference: 'Portals are for visiting, platforms are for building on' (Sherratt, 2013). These digital collections, like Hathi Trust Digital Library or Old Bailey Online, all provide application programming interfaces (APIs) that allow users to bypass the search interface and work directly with the archive's text or underlying metadata, or using third-party tools that are linked via the collection's website to analyse or transform that material. Both Gale Primary Sources and Gale Digital Scholar Lab exemplify the figurative and computational senses of the term: they are platforms in the sense of an architecture upon which stand a large number of Gale's digital collections. Gale Primary Sources was described as an 'Enhanced product platform', but they both also offer applications to analyse the texts; the Lab offers tools and third-party applications and is described as a 'text and data mining platform' (Houghton & Ketchley, 2019: 5; Rand & Fust, 2019).

This is perhaps the most radical departure from bookishness for ECCO's books since both platforms were explicitly designed to enhance the analysis of the OCR text in the light of digital humanities and computer-aided quantitative analysis, popularly known as 'distant reading' after Franco Moretti's work (also known as text analysis, text mining, or macro-analysis) (Gale, 2016, 2018). The earliest use of computers in humanities scholarship was for linguistic analysis and electronic concordances, such as Father Roberto Busa's computer index to Thomas Aquinas' *Summa Theologiae*, begun in 1949 with IBM. Busa is generally cited as the seminal figure in humanities computing (Wisbey, 1962: 163–7; Hockey, 2004: 3–19). However, the increasing availability of very large collections and archives of digitised text by the early twenty-first century meant that the 'number-crunching abilities of the computer' could be 'set free to perform

---

[64] Historical Texts, https://historicaltexts.Jisc.ac.uk/ [accessed 27 July 2020].

quantitative analyses that shed light on the text's authorship, style, genre, theme, plot, even ideology' on an 'unprecedented scale' (Hammond, 2016: 83; Jockers, 2013, 27).

In 2013–14 Gale launched two initiatives to make its digitised collections more amenable to such techniques and tools. One was by selling TDMs to subscribing libraries, essentially a terabyte hard drive that contained the XML files of the metadata and the OCR text (Gale, 2014). The other was the roll-out of a new interface to some of Gale's collections, including ECCO, called 'Artemis', which allowed the user to directly see and work with the OCR text using built-in tools for word frequency analysis and visualisation (Gale, 2013). Artemis was short-lived and was rapidly replaced in 2016 by Gale Primary Sources. While we've seen how the TDM drives have been problematic for libraries, the initiative was Gale's response to digital scholarship. Chris Houghton (Gale's head of digital scholarship,), discussed in an email interview what led to the development of the Gale Digital Scholar Lab:

> Beginning in the early 2010s, Gale had been receiving requests to access the underlying data for our archives, either OCR or metadata. These requests led us into conversations with academics, predominantly in the Digital Humanities space, which meant that as an organisation, we started to get a better idea about the community, the networks, and most importantly, the research. We tried to be as open as possible to these requests for data.

One of the results, he notes, was that 'we made the conscious decision to be brave and really lift the lid on Gale's OCR process' on the new interfaces. The perception of the open culture of digital humanities was perceived to go hand in hand with scholars' need to work directly with the OCR text and metadata of Gale's digital collections: 'We knew that the community prized openness and accessibility, which would automatically clash with the fact that our archives are behind paywalls, so we came to the conclusion that we would try and make as much of the platform as open and visible as possible, allowing users to extract data and analyses at every stage' (Houghton,

2019). Gale's hope was that the sophisticated capabilities of its latest interface to its digital collections like ECCO would somehow mitigate or offset the effect of paywalled access.

Gale has certainly worked at being more transparent about what is involved in digitisation. On the Gale Primary Sources public page there is a now a 'Behind the Scenes' page with an article entitled 'Creating a Digital Archive: The Technical Processes' which takes us through the basics aspects of image capture, OCR, metadata, XML, quality assurance, and last 'the application' (in other words the interface).[65] In parallel, both of the latest interfaces to Gale's digital archives offer the ability to open a side window to see the OCR'd text accompanying the page image.[66] Both also offer a screen-tip that explains 'How this text was created' which notes factors that affect OCR confidence, including the 'condition of the original document', whether it is handwritten or printed, the date the document was created (this seems to mean when the remediated document was created), the scanning equipment, and the 'Maturity of the OCR algorithm used at the time of creation'. Moreover, each document's text comes with a figure that represents the OCR engine's 'confidence in the accuracy of the conversion from image to text'. The visibility of the OCR confidence figure is potentially useful. One study has found that, while ECCO's figures are on the whole higher than other calculations, there was a general correlation between Gale's figures and those of the study, indicating that, relatively speaking, this 'supports being able to use the OCR engine confidence value to accurately assess OCR quality' (Tolonen, Mäkelä, Ijaz, & Lahti, forthcoming 2021). However, ECCO II OCR confidence figures are lower than for ECCO I (Tolonen et al., forthcoming 2021). This is probably because they are calculated in different ways by the two different OCR engines:

---

[65] Behind the Scenes at Gale: Creating a Digital Archive. www.gale.com/intl/archives-explored/behind-the-scenes/creating-a-digital-archive-technical [accessed 25 May 2020].

[66] Jisc Historical Texts also makes the OCR text visible; it also uses ECCO-TCP transcribed text where that is available.

PrimeRecognition was used on ECCO I in 2003; ABBYY was used for ECCO II in 2009.[67]

The text analysis tools on the Lab platform are powerful and capable of tracing highly suggestive topical and linguistic patterns. The platform offers tools for cleaning the OCR text, word frequency counting (ngrams), document clustering, topic modelling, sentiment analysis, and natural language processing. In addition, all the tools are capable of producing data in the form of spreadsheets or various kinds of graphic visualisation. However, the increased focus on the *text* of the books in ECCO risks bypassing the bookishness of books, those eccentricities introduced by the handmade processes of book production and transmission. This shift can be traced in the presentation of metadata on these two platforms.

In Gale Primary Sources the reader can choose to prioritise page images or text, or have the page image surrounded by text, a table of contents, an 'explore' window (a facility to search the text of the book), or bibliographical metadata ('full citation'). Curiously, metadata is split between two different views. The first, in the 'explore' view, contains a link that opens up a pop-up window listing the holding libraries, a brief note about pagination, and what to many must be an obscure reference, 'Moore, 68' (Figure 22).[68] There is also an option to see the *Essay* alongside an expanded set of metadata (Figure 23).

It is not clear why different facets of the book's metadata are split across separate windows. Neither is it clear for whom this selection of metadata is intended: the Gale ID seems to look towards internal systems; some of the bibliographical metadata is very specialised (e.g. 'Moore, 68', or the microfilm reel number), while some is suppressed (no LoC subject headings); and

---

[67] ABBYY outlines how a confidence score is calculated. ABBYY – Character Confidence, https://support.abbyy.com/hc/en-us/articles/360004745639-CharConfidence-and-IsSuspicious-difference [accessed 10 March 2020].

[68] This is a remnant of the methodology behind the ESTC: where possible a reference to a scholarly bibliographical study was included; in this case, J. R. Moore's 1960 *A Checklist of the Writings of Daniel Defoe*, p. 58.

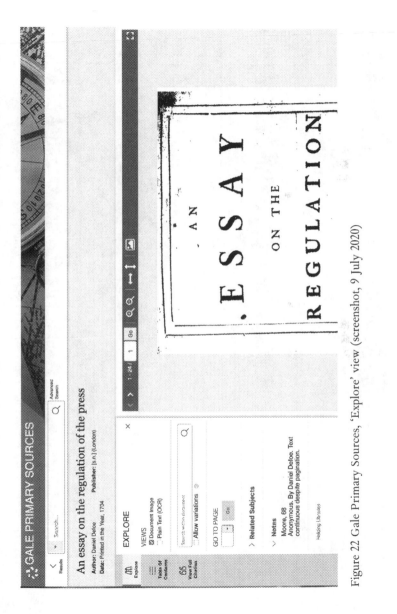

Figure 22 Gale Primary Sources, 'Explore' view (screenshot, 9 July 2020)

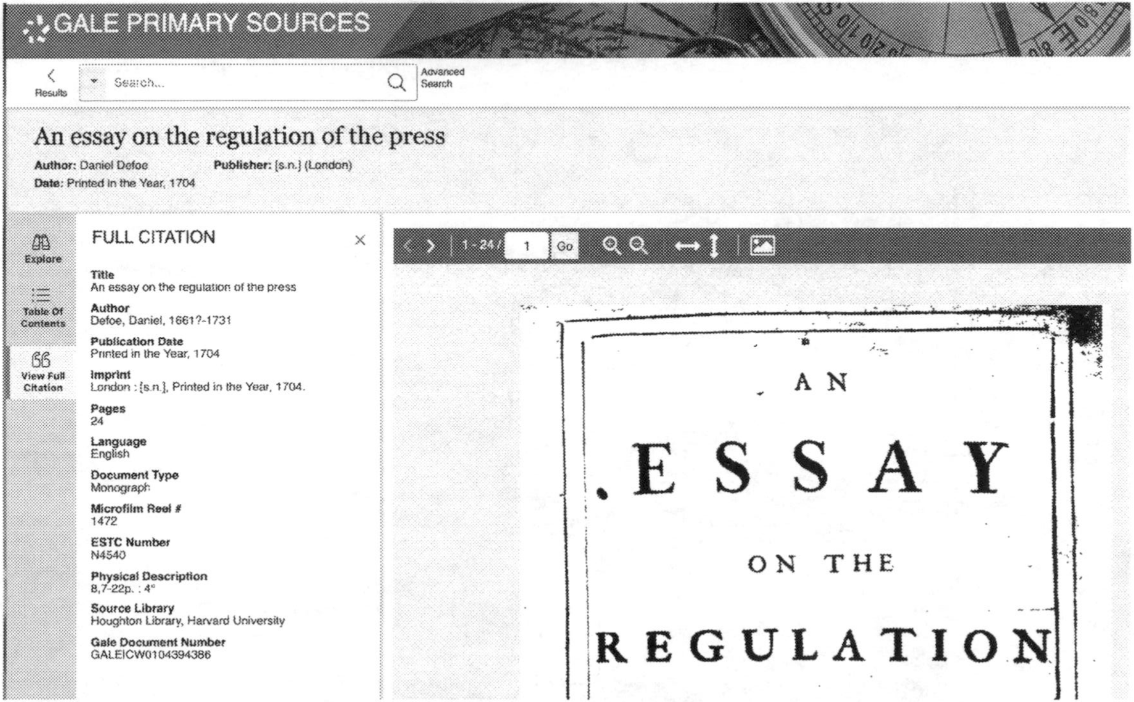

Figure 23 Gale Primary Sources, 'Full Citation' view (screenshot, 9 July 2020)

MANAGE | ANALYZE

Search within results

Limit Search by:

Archives ⌄
Eighteenth Century C... (3)

Content Type ⌄
Monograph (3)

Document Type ⌄
Monograph (3)

Publication Dates: ⌄
From
To
Search

Publication Title ⌄
Literature and Langu... (3)

Publication Languages ⌄
English (3)

Add to Content Set · Remove from Content Set · Search History

Search Terms:
Document Title (The works of Alexander Pope, Esq; Vol. I. With explanatory notes and additions never before printed)

☐ Select All

1

☐ The works of Alexander Pope, Esq; Vol. I. With explanatory notes and additions never before printed
BY Alexander Pope
OCR CONFIDENCE 93% ☺
A DISCOURSE ON PASTORAL POETRY. T H E R E are not, I believe, a greater number of any fort of verses than of those which are called Paftorals; nor a fmaller, than of those which are truly so. It therefore feems neceff...

ARCHIVE	Eighteenth Century Collections Online
SOURCE LIBRARY	British Library
CONTENT TYPE	Monograph
DOCUMENT TYPE	Monograph
PUBLICATION DATE	1736
PUBLICATION	Literature and Language I.
PUBLISHER	Gale.

☐ The works of Alexander Pope, Esq; Vol. I. With explanatory notes and additions never before printed
BY Alexander Pope
OCR CONFIDENCE 93%
A. DISCOURSE ON PASTORAL POETRY. H E R E are not, I believe, a greater number of any fort of verses than of those which are called Paftorals ; nor a smaller, than of those which are truly so. It therefore seems neceff...

ARCHIVE	Eighteenth Century Collections Online
SOURCE LIBRARY	British Library
CONTENT TYPE	Monograph
DOCUMENT TYPE	Monograph
PUBLICATION DATE	1736
PUBLICATION	Literature and Language I.
PUBLISHER	Gale.

☐ The works of Alexander Pope, Esq; Vol. I. With explanatory notes and additions never before printed
BY Alexander Pope
OCR CONFIDENCE 94%
PASTORALS. WITH A DISCOURSE on PASTORAL. Written in the Year 1704. Rura mihi & rigui placeant in vallibus amnes, Flumina amem, fbvafhæ, inglorius I VIRG, Ve L.. B A DISCOURSE N PASTORAL POETRY T H E R E are not, I...

ARCHIVE	Eighteenth Century Collections Online
SOURCE LIBRARY	Bodleian Library, University of Oxford
CONTENT TYPE	Monograph
DOCUMENT TYPE	Monograph
PUBLICATION DATE	1736
PUBLICATION	Literature and Language I.
PUBLISHER	Gale.

Figure 24 Gale Digital Scholar Lab, search results list (screenshot, 1 June 2020)

the document type 'monograph' might be of utility to a library cataloguer but likely not to a scholar or student.

The way in which Gale Digital Scholar Lab presents a book's metadata is again different. It includes only basic metadata of author, title, and imprint, Gale's document identification, a link path to ECCO, and the date of access. The source library is indicated in the results page, but all other material traces of the book – the bibliographical metadata accumulated by the ESTC – have not been included. This means that, for example, if we wanted to search for the particular edition of Alexander Pope's *Works* (1736), for which I examined the title page to volume one in my earlier section on bookishness, we can see that ECCO digitised three copies. Each has small material differences; the ESTC records these differences and allocates them individual ESTC identification numbers. However, since the Lab platform does not reproduce this, it's very difficult to tell which particular copy is which (Figure 24).

Bibliographical metadata is also there to help us decode or add material context to what cannot be seen in the image. In the example of the title page to volume one of the *Works*, there is no bibliographical metadata, no indication at all, that the title page is in fact printed in red and black ink (Figure 13). So, while clearly extending the capabilities of computing power to analyse text, the Lab has returned us to a state before ECCO where image and bibliographical metadata are separated. This also parallels some of the conceptions of distant reading, which, as Katherine Bode has pointed out, conceives text as the be-all and end-all, in which works are perceived as 'singular and stable entities' abstracted from the medium of their transmission – the book. Bode contrasts this perception with an understanding of the works as 'events – unfolding and accruing meaning across time and space – and the documentary record as partially and provisionally expressing that process' (Bode, 2019: 5). In short, the platform risks the very abstraction that Robin Alston, the editor of the 18thC STC, worried about when negotiating between the organisation of data required by computerised cataloguing systems and the 'eccentric evidence' of books produced by hand-press (Alston, 1981a: 379). Jisc's Historical Texts, Gale Primary Sources, and Gale Digital Scholar Lab are designed to offer libraries access to cross-searchable packages of different digital collections, each of which were created differently and with different metadata. Standardising how metadata was represented in these platforms was an understandable and challenging priority for Jisc and Gale. In addition, the age of quantitative analysis has radically shifted the priorities of how a book is understood and interrogated. These factors are clearly reflected in the decreasing coherence and detail of bibliographical metadata and an increased focus on *text* in these platforms.

In addition, the subsuming of individual collections like ECCO within a single platform homogenises the nature of these heterogeneous collections. The history of each collection's creation will be different and exerts a decisive – if sometimes obscure – force on the nature of the collections. In a recent study researchers compared the entire ECCO corpus to the most accurate data of the print culture of the period, the ESTC, in order to assess the issue of representativeness (ECCO includes around 50 per cent of what is in the ESTC). However, the study found a number of 'clear biases in the collection' that are a result of its 'complicated provenance' (Tolonen et al., forthcoming 2021). For example, it notes that material printed in America is under-represented relative to material printed in England, Scotland, Ireland, France, and other countries, and perhaps unsurprisingly, works in the English language dominate both ECCO and the ESTC (although ECCO includes a large proportion of works in Welsh). Moreover, the distribution of texts from across the century is biased: ECCO contains far more works from 1780–90 and 1790–1800 than from earlier decades. Complicating this distribution is the presence of reprints of existing works, which represent a significant proportion of the total works in ECCO, and which vary from 20–25 per cent in the first decade of the century to 30–35 per cent between 1730 and 1790. Overall, these biases amplify each other and therefore crucially affect searches performed on ECCO's interfaces (Tolonen et al., forthcoming 2021).[69]

But the concerns of bibliography that are a result of ECCO's 'complicated provenance' are also connected to the politics of representation, and we must attend to the cultural resonances of digital collections and

[69] See also May (2009).

their interfaces. Gillespie's final meaning of 'platform' builds on the figurative and architectural: it is *political*, in the sense that a political organisation or politician might take a stand on or take up a position in relation to a certain issue (Gillespie, 2010: 350). This last meaning makes visible a tension within the idea of the platform: that it is at once a democratic, neutral, open space and a space that enables a particular position to be taken up, a space that is implicitly hierarchical or even exclusionary (Gillespie, 2010: 350–1; Thylstrup, 2018: 126–31).

Archives, as Trouillot remind us, are sites of power and also silence (Trouillot, 1995: 26). The urgent debates within the field of digital humanities have sought to reveal the silences of digital scholarship and how digitisation projects tended to replicate 'a canon that skews toward traditional texts and excludes crucial work by women, people of color, and the GLBTQ community' (Earhart, 2012). As Tim Sherratt argues:

> Online collections have a history. Digital access is the product of analogue processes – of institutional policies and individual judgements. Our search results are not manufactured by algorithms alone. They are created by many small acts of human imagination, initiative, obstruction and neglect. (Sherratt, 2019: 5)

The prehistory of ECCO was, perhaps unsurprisingly, inflected by the cultural values present during the heyday of the massive cataloguing and microfilming projects of the twentieth century. Molly Hardy, reflecting on the records of African-American printers, reminds us that cataloguing is 'built out of and therefore reflects on a particular moment', and Tim Hitchcock highlights how the major commercial online collections are shaped by their dependence on microfilm collections whose selection criteria reflected the value placed on 'male and European culture' (Hardy, 2016; Hitchcock, 2016). The 18thC STC was an Anglo-American collaboration that projected a distinctly Anglocentric printed world. The decision for its geographical and linguistic focus was certainly driven by understandable, pragmatic reasons of scope and cost, but the 18thC STC as a whole was also shaped by the idea, as Alston put it, of a 'national bibliographical record' (quoted in Crump, in Snyder 2003: 49). Moreover, the initial phase of microfilming by RPI selected twenty-eight 'major authors' deemed worthy to have every variant and edition filmed, and who are therefore disproportionately represented in ECCO.[70] The linguistic and geographical bias has its basis in the catalogue, but the effect of this is amplified by the initial emphasis on canonical authors – all male and all white – originating in the filming programme.

Nevertheless, access is not just about content, but also about what users can do with the content. As Roopika Risam argued, '[t]he reification of canons in digital form is not only a function of *what* is there – what gets digitalized and thus represented in the digital cultural record – but also *how* it is there' (Risam, 2018: 17). For instance, the affordances of digitisation might offer ways of aiding the discoverability of voices obscured by the originary biases of digital collections by leveraging how texts and their metadata are organised, searched, and analysed (Koh, 2014: 388; Risam, 2015). This arguably is what the platform might enable. The cross-searchable platform and the aggregation of different collections that include those with a wider linguistic and global scope is a potential means to ameliorate the biases of individual collections. In addition, while the Gale Primary Sources and Gale Digital Scholar Lab obscures the bookishness of old books, their focus on other forms of organising and discovering – in particular, the emphasis on text mining, visualisation, and machine-aided indexing – might be more sympathetic to the aims of postcolonial and intersectional digital humanities practices.

The platforms that give access to ECCO produce ambivalent effects. On one hand, they can leverage powerful tools for discoverability and, in some cases, analysis of hidden voices. To an extent this could mitigate biases

---

[70] ECCO – Research Tools – Origins and Contexts, http://find.gale.com.bathspa .idm.oclc.org/ecco/researchTools [accessed 11 May 2020]. See also Primary Source Media- Eighteenth Century – Collection Information, http://micro formguides.gale.com/Data/Introductions/20190FM.htm [accessed 26 July 2019].

hidden within the prehistory of individual collections of old books. However, the emphasis on text analysis comes at the cost of the material life of old books; subsumed within the platform, the material prehistory of collections like ECCO risks being lost.

6 Conclusion

ECCO is still changing. From 2020 Gale started a huge expansion to ECCO by new colour imaging of missing editions and titles, adding around 90,000 texts. This comprises titles added to the ESTC after 2009, some missed in ECCO I and II, and some missing from Evan's Early American Imprints database (de Mowbray, 2020b). One wonders what effect 'ECCO phase III' will have on the eventual nature of ECCO. Given that the colour digitisation will be of the actual books (rather than the low black-and-white fidelity of microfilm), it will be a boon to those interested in the 'bookishness' of books, and direct imaging may also benefit the accuracy of the OCR. In addition, there are projects working in collaboration with Gale to attempt to improve the OCR text, such as the Computational History group at the University of Helsinki, and collaborative efforts sparked by the 2018 report 'A Research Agenda for Historical and Multilingual Optical Character Recognition' (Smith & Cordell, 2018). And of course, going by the past evidence, ECCO will continue to evolve. The digital collection so many of us rely upon has been and will continue to be a mutable artefact.

It is for this reason that the book is a 'history' or even a life history: ECCO inherited decisions made by its antecedents. This is borne out by the decisive effect the 18thC STC and the microfilm collection had on ECCO. The massive digital cataloguing of early print that started with the 18thC STC in 1978 and continued with the ESTC exemplified how metadata could be searched and queried in new and sophisticated ways. But the records themselves were ultimately the product of human interpretation and fallibility: how would the uniqueness of hand-press books be translated in standardised data? This metadata – now deeply embedded in ECCO – defines, to a significant degree, how ECCO is searched and how texts might be discovered. The 18thC STC also defined the linguistic and geographical limits of the printed material that currently exists in ECCO; it was an

Anglocentric canon arguably amplified by the subsequent microfilm collection, Research Publications' The Eighteenth Century. While H. G. Wells envisioned a world of universal access to knowledge, the knowledge disseminated was based on the archives of the West, and that access was enabled by applying a new technology to a new model of publishing dominated by commercial publishers based in the United States and the United Kingdom. The significance of this shouldn't be underestimated since the techno-commercial model of microfilm access would be the basis of the earliest and largest digital library resources of early print, and form the future of how commercial publishers leveraged new technologies in the age of online resources. Of course, that model did not go unquestioned, and Gale sought to ameliorate concerns about access and at the same time to expand the reach of ECCO by various licensing deals and the development if its platforms. That those same platforms conceal as much as they reveal should also alert us to how techno-commercial decisions shape both what we can access and how we can use that access.

Part of my argument is that our apprehension of why ECCO works the way it does involves understanding how its present echoes its past (you'll forgive the pun). Once we recognise that digital resources, collections, and archives are not static, that they have a history, then we can begin to excavate that history. Moreover, it is a material history: it involves changes in technology, cultural factors, and commercial forces. If the aim of bibliography is to tell the material life history of a book – including all the cultural, institutional, and technological forces acting upon it – in other words, a 'sociology of books' (McKenzie, 1999: 12–15), then this propels us to also consider the material life history of digital resources in the same way. In this sense my book is a case study of a methodology for the study of digital archives, the application – the aptness – of bibliography to digital resources.

But the other part of my argument concerns the necessity to do this kind of history. Ryan Cordell usefully relates the '*understandable*' decisions institutions, companies, and even individuals make, to the necessity for us to have '*understood*' these since they provide 'essential context' for the work we do with books and digital resources (Cordell, 2017: 207). Now more than ever, it is important for us to understand the history and nature of digital collections created in the late 1990s and early 2000s as they become subsumed within the platform. As we've seen, that history can be hidden by commercial exigencies, simple human fallibility, or the geo-cultural politics of power. When I started, I had in the back of my mind the vintage Ladybird book series 'How It Works' as a model for understanding and revealing this history of ECCO. But more seriously, I argue that we cannot afford to be naïve about our digital resources. When we are increasingly dependent upon digital resources for our studies, whether we are a student or scholar, we cannot do this without understanding the contours of what we depend upon, and what we can and cannot do with old books. If nothing else, I hope my history might begin to help us to become better, more critically nuanced users of the platforms of the future.

References

Albanese, A. (2010) BiblioBazaar: How a Company Produces 272,930 Books a Year. *Publisher's Weekly*, www.publishersweekly.com/pw/by-topic/industry-news/publisher-news/article/42850-bibliobazaar-how-a-company-produces-272–930-books-a-year.html (Accessed 10 May 2020).

Alston, R. (1981a) Computers and Bibliography: The New Approach in ESTC. *The Papers of the Bibliographical Society of America*. 75. 371–89.

Alston, R. (1981b) ESTC Texts on Microfilm. *Factotum: Newsletter of the XVIIIth Century STC* (no. 12). 2–3.

Alston, R. (2004) The History of ESTC. *Age of Johnson*. 15, https://web.archive.org/web/20090518013849/ http://www.r-alston.co.uk:80/review.htm (Accessed 22 June 2018).

Alston, R. & Janetta, M. J. (1978) *Bibliography, Machine-Readable Cataloguing, and the ESTC*. London: The British Library.

Anon. (2003) Eighteenth Century Collections Online. *Booklist* (no. 5).

Ashby, P. & Campbell, R. (1979) *Microform Publishing*. London: Butterworths.

Aw, G. (2007) Got ECCO? Literature Compass MLA Panel 2007, www.youtube.com/watch?v=MA1KJjSYba8 (Accessed 19 December 2019).

Baker, J. (2016) Interfaces between Us and Our Digital Sources. *Cradledincaricature*, https://cradledincaricature.com/2016/04/06/interfaces-between-us-and-our-digital-sources/ (Accessed 22 June 2018).

Baker, N. (2001) *Double Fold: Libraries and the Assault on Paper*. New York: Random House.

Battigelli, A. (2010) ASECS Summary of 'Some Noisy Feedback' Roundtable, Albuquerque, 18 March. *Early Modern Online Bibliography*, https://earlymodernonlinebib.wordpress.com/2010/03/27/asecs-summary-of-some-noisy-feedback-roundtable-albuquerque-31810/ (Accessed 19 May 2020).

Battin, P. (1988) NHA Testimony: Patricia M. Battin, 17 March 1988, https://web.archive.org/web/20061003232933/ http://www.nhalliance.org/testimony/1988/88testimony-pbattin.html (Accessed 20 May 2020).

Benjamin, W. (1970) *Illuminations*. H. Arendt (ed.) Bungay: Jonathan Cape.

Berger, S. E. (2019) Endleaves. In D. Duncan & A. Smyth (eds.) *Book Parts*. Oxford: Oxford University Press. pp. 277–85.

Berry, J. (2004) New Products & Vision. *Library Journal*. 129 (13). 19–19.

Binkley, R. C. (1931) *Methods of Reproducing Research Materials: A Survey Made for the Joint Committee on Materials for Research of the Social Science Research Council and the American Council of Learned Societies*. Ann Arbor, MI: Edwards Brothers. Hathi Trust Digital Library, http://hdl.handle.net/2027/mdp.39015041315394 (Accessed 26 April 2019).

Binkley, R. C. (1936) *Manual on Methods of Reproducing Research Materials: A Survey Made for the Joint Committee on Materials for Research of the Social Science Research Council and the American Council of Learned Societies*. Ann Arbor, MI: Edwards Brothers. Hathi Trust Digital Library, http://hdl.handle.net/2027/mdp.39015003329243 (Accessed 26 April 2019).

Binkley, R. C. (1935/1948) New Tools for Men of Letters. In M. H. Fisch (ed.) *Selected Papers of Robert C. Binkley*. Cambridge, MA: Harvard University Press. pp. 179–97, www.wallandbinkley.com/rcb/works/new-tools-for-men-of-letters.html (Accessed 23 February 2020).

Bode, K. (2019) *A World of Fiction: Digital Collections and the Future of Literary History*. Ann Arbor: University of Michigan Press.

Borsuk, A. (2018) *The Book*. Cambridge, MA: MIT Press.

Bourne, C. P. & Hahn, T. B. (2003) *A History of Online Information Services, 1963–1976*. Cambridge, MA: MIT Press.

Bower, J. L. & Christensen, C. M. (1995) Disruptive Technologies: Catching the Wave. *Harvard Business Review* (no. 1). 43–53.

Centrelli, K. (2012) ECCO on JISC and Contextual Word Searches. *The Long Eighteenth*, https://long18th.wordpress.com/2012/04/10/ecco-on-jisc-and-contextual-word-searches/ (Accessed 28 July 2018).

Chadwyck-Healey, C. (2020) *Publishing for Libraries at the Dawn of the Digital Age*. London: Bloomsbury.

Cordell, R. (2017) 'Q i-jtb the Raven': Taking Dirty OCR Seriously. *Book History*. 20 (1). 188–225.

Crump, M. (1988) Why Eighteenth-Century Short Titles Are Long. *Factotum: Newsletter of the XVIIIth Century STC* (no. 26). July. 5–6.

Crump, M. (2003) The Origins of the ESTC: The Case for Vision. In H. Snyder & M. S. Smith (eds.) *The English Short Title Catalogue: Past, Present, Future*. New York: AMS Press. pp. 45–63.

Dane, J. (2012) *What Is a Book? The Study of Early Printed Books*. Notre Dame, IN: University of Notre Dame Press.

Darnton, R. (2012) Digitize, Democratize: Libraries and the Future of Books. *Columbia Journal of Law & the Arts*. 1 (1). 1–20.

De Bolla, P. (2013) *The Architecture of Concepts: The Historical Formation of Human Rights*. New York: Fordham University Press.

Deegan, M. & Sutherland, K. (2009) *Transferred Illusions: Digital Technology and the Forms of Print*. Aldershot: Ashgate.

Defoe, D (2010) *An Essay on the Regulation of the Press*. Charleston, SC: BiblioLife.

Earhart, A. E. (2012) 'Can Information Be Unfettered? Race and the New Digital Humanities Canon', in *Debates in the Digital Humanities*, https://dhdebates.gc.cuny.edu/read/untitled-88c11800-9446-469b-a3be-3fdb36bfbd1e/section/cf0af04d-73e3-4738-98d9-74c1ae3534e5 (Accessed 23 July 2020).

Emerson, L. (2014) *Reading Writing Interfaces: From the Digital to the Bookbound*. Minneapolis: University of Minnesota Press.

Enis, M. (2014) Gale Founder Frederick Ruffner Dies at 88. *Library Journal*, www.libraryjournal.com?detailStory=gale-founder-frederick-ruffner-dies-at-88 (Accessed 6 September 2019).

Eve, M. P. (2014) *Open Access and the Humanities: Contexts, Controversies and the Future*. Cambridge: Cambridge University Press.

Factotum: Newsletter of the XVIIIth century STC, ed. J. L. Wood. London: British Library. March 1978 to December 1995.

Findlay, P. (2019) Library Collections: Navigating the Payment for Access Minefield, www.jisc.ac.uk/blog/library-collections-navigating-the-payment-for-access-minefield-09-sep–2019. (accessed 4 March 2020).

Fitzpatrick, K. (2011) *Planned Obsolescence: Publishing, Technology, and the Future of the Academy*. New York: New York University Press.

Gadd, I. (2009) The Use and Misuse of Early English Books Online. *Literature Compass*. 6 (3). 680–92.

Gale (2004) ECCO User's Guide. Brochure.

Gale (2010) Gale and 18thConnect Partner to Improve Access to Eighteenth Century Documents, https://news.cengage.com/library-research/gale-and-18thconnect-partner-to-improve-access-to-eighteenth-century-documents/ (Accessed 23 January 2020).

Gale (2013) Gale to Unify the Humanities through Artemis, https://news.cengage.com/higher-education/gale-to-unify-the-humanities-through-artemis/ (Accessed 23 January 2020).

Gale (2014) Data Mining the Gale Digital Collections. Frequently Asked Questions. Brochure. assets.cengage.com/pdf/faq_DataMining.PDF (accessed 21 January 2020).

Gale (2016) Continuing the Tradition with Gale Primary Sources, https://blog.gale.com/continuing-the-tradition-with-gale-primary-sources/ (Accessed 23 January 2020).

Gale (2018) Gale Transforms Digital Humanities Research with Launch of New Digital Scholar Lab, https://news.cengage.com/library-research/

gale-transforms-digital-humanities-research-with-launch-of-new-digi
tal-scholar-lab/ (Accessed 23 January 2020).

Galey, A. (2012) Openings. *ArchBook: Architectures of the Book*,
https://drc.usask.ca/projects/archbook/openings.php (Accessed
11 March 2020).

Garrett, J. (2007) Subject Headings in Full-Text Environments: The
ECCO Experiment. *College and Research Libraries*. 68 (1). 69–81.

Gavin, M. (2019) How to Think about EEBO. *Textual Cultures*. 11 (1–2).
70–105.

Gillespie, T. (2010) The Politics of 'Platforms'. *New Media & Society*. 12
(3). 347–64.

Gitelman, L. (2014) *Paper Knowledge: Toward a Media History of
Documents*. Durham, NC: Duke University Press.

Golderman, G. & Connolly, B. (2008) Oldies but Goodies. *Library Journal*.
18–26.

Greenfield, S. (2009) Undergraduate Use of Search Engines in EEBO and
ECCO. *The Eighteenth-Century Intelligencer*. 23 (3). 13–16.

Greenfield, S. (2010) ECCO OCR Troubleshooting. *Early Modern Online
Bibliography*, https://earlymodernonlinebib.wordpress.com/ecco-ocr-
troubleshooting-by-sayre-greenfield/ (Accessed 22 June 2018).

Greetham, D. C. (1994) *Textual Scholarship: An Introduction*. New York:
Garland.

Greg, W. W. (1945) Bibliography: A Retrospect. In F. C. Francis (ed.). *The
Bibliographical Society, 1892–1941: Studies in Retrospect*. London:
Bibliographical Society. pp. 23–31.

Gregg, S. (2007) Using Eighteenth-Century Collections Online (ECCO) As a
Learning and Teaching Resource. *English Subject Centre Archive*, http://
english.heacademy.ac.uk/2016/01/16/using-eighteenth-century-collec
tions-online-as-a-learning-and-teaching-resource/ (Accessed 3 September
2019).

Gregg, S. (2012) Digital Humanities and Archives @ ASECS 2012. *Manicule*, https://shgregg.com/2012/04/05/digital-humanities-and-archives-asecs-2012–3/ (Accessed 19 December 2019).

Gregg, S. (2016) 1748: 'Fiction' in the Database. *Manicule*. https://shgregg.com/2016/03/24/1748-fiction-in-the-database/ (Accessed 21 October 2020).

Gregg, S. (2017/2019) Finding ECCO-TCP Texts. *Manicule*, https://shgregg.com/2017/08/16/finding-ecco-tcp-texts/ (Accessed 31 May 2020).

Hammond, A. (2016) *Literature in the Digital Age: An Introduction.* Cambridge: Cambridge University Press.

Hane, P. (2004) Thomson Gale Upgrades the Learning Experience [online]. Available from: www.infotoday.com/IT/jun04/hane1.shtml (Accessed 5 September 2019).

Hardy, M. O. (2016) '"Black Printers" on White Cards: Information Architecture in the Data Structures of the Early American Book Trades'. In *Debates in the Digital Humanities*, https://dhdebates.gc.cuny.edu/read/untitled/section/3c4a647f-8f61-48b6-ab41-5d6e765ac70f#ch31 (Accessed 21 July 2020).

Harris, P. R. (1998) *A History of the British Museum, 1753–1973.* London: British Library.

Helmond, A. (2015) The Platformization of the Web: Making Web Data Platform Ready. *Social Media + Society*. 1 (2). 825–43.

Hill, M. J. & Hengchen, S. (2019) Quantifying the Impact of Dirty OCR on Historical Text Analysis: Eighteenth Century Collections Online As a Case Study. *Digital Scholarship in the Humanities*. 34 (4). 824–43.

Hine, I. (2016) Experimenting with the Imperfect: ECCO & OCR. *Linguistic DNA*, www.linguisticdna.org/ecco-ocr/ (Accessed 31 July 2020).

Hitchcock, T. (2016) Digital Humanities in Three Dimensions. *Historyonics*, https://historyonics.blogspot.com/2016/07/the-digital-humanities-in-three.html (Accessed 5 March 2020).

Hockey, S. (2004) The History of Humanities Computing. In S. Schreibman, R. Siemans, & J. Unsworth (eds.) *A Companion to Digital Humanities*. Oxford: Blackwell. pp. 3–19.

Holley, R. (2009) How Good Can It Get? Analysing and Improving OCR Accuracy in Large Scale Historic Newspaper Digitization Programs. *D-Lib Magazine*. 15 (3/4), www.dlib.org/dlib/march09/holley/03hol ley.html (Accessed 18 December 2019).

Houghton, C. & Ketchley, S. (2019) From Provider to Partner: How Digital Humanities Sparked a Change in Gale's Relationship with Universities. *Insights*. 32 (1), 1–9.

Jackson, W. (1941) Some Limitations of Microfilm. *The Papers of the Bibliographical Society of America*. 35. 281–8.

Jockers, M. (2013) *Macroanalysis: Digital Methods and Literary History*. Urbana: University of Illinois Press.

Johnston, L. (2012) Before You Were Born: We Were Digitizing Texts. *The Signal*. //blogs.loc.gov/thesignal/2012/12/before-you-were-born-we-were-digitizing-texts/ (Accessed 20 July 2020).

Kirschenbaum, M. & Werner, S. (2014) Digital Scholarship and Digital Studies: The State of the Discipline. *Book History*. 17. 406–58.

Koh, A. (2014) Inspecting the Nineteenth-Century Literary Digital Archive: Omissions of Empire. *Journal of Victorian Culture*. 19 (3). 385–95.

Levack, K. (2003) Digital ECCOs of the Eighteenth Century. *EContent*. 26 (11). 36–9.

Liu, A. (2013) Imagining the New Media Encounter. In R. Siemans & S. Schriebman (eds.) *A Companion to Digital Literary Studies*. Chichester: Wiley Blackwell. pp. 3–15.

Lockhart, V. & Swartzell, A. (1990) Evaluation of Microfilm Vendors. *Microform Review*. 19 (3). 119–23.

Mak, B. (2014) Archaeology of a Digitization. *Journal of the Association for Information Science & Technology*. 65 (8). 1515–26.

Mandell, L. (2011) TCP and Gale Cengage Release 2,200 ECCO Texts to the Public. *18thConnect*, www.18thconnect.org/news/?p=49 (Accessed 27 February 2019).

Mandell, L. (2012a) Brave New World: A Look at 18thConnect. *Age of Johnson*. 15. 299–309.

Mandell, L. (2012b) Mellon Foundation Grant Proposal, https://emop .tamu.edu/about (Accessed 16 March 2020).

Mandell, L. (2012c) Mellon Foundation Grant Proposal: Appendix,: https://emop.tamu.edu/about (Accessed 16 March 2020).

Mandell, L. (2015) eMOP Mellon Final Report, https://emop.tamu.edu/ about (Accessed 16 January 2020).

Mandell, L. & Grumbach, E. (2015) The Business of Digital Humanities: Capitalism and Enlightenment. *Scholarly and Research Communication*. 6 (4), https://src-online.ca/src/index.php/src/article/view/226 (Accessed 22 June 2018).

Martin, S. (2007) EEBO, Microfilm, and Umberton Eco: Historical Lessons and Future Directions for Electronic Collections. *Microform and Imaging Review*. 36 (4). 159–64.

Martin, S. (2009) A Universal Humanities Digital Library: Pipe Dream or Prospective Future? In M. M. Deyrup (ed.) *Digital Scholarship*. Abingdon: Routledge. pp. 1–12.

Mattern, S. (2014) Library As Infrastructure. *Places Journal*, https:// placesjournal.org/article/library-as-infrastructure/ (Accessed 26 May 2020).

May, J. (2009) Some Problems in ECCO (and ESTC). *Eighteenth-Century Intelligencer*. 23 (1). 20–30.

McCracken, J. (1998) Gale Research to Merge: Parent Firm Forms $350 m Research Unit. *Crain's Detroit Business*, www.crainsdetroit .com/article/19980921/SUB/809210874/gale-research-to-merge-par ent-firm-forms-350m-research-unit (Accessed 31 July 2019).

McKenzie, D. F. (1999) *Bibliography and the Sociology of Texts*. Cambridge: Cambridge University Press.

McKitterick, D. (2013) *Old Books, New Technologies: The Representation, Conservation and Transformation of Books since 1700*. Cambridge: Cambridge University Press.

Meckler, A. M. (1982) *Micropublishing: A History of Scholarly Micropublishing in America, 1938–1980*. Westport, CT: Greenwood Press.

Milloy, C. (2012) Changing the Face of Scholarly Information Provision: A Case Study of Developing and Launching JISC eCollections. *Insights*. 25 (1). 74–9. http://insights.uksg.org/articles/10.1629/2048–7754.25.1.74/ (Accessed 25 January 2019).

Nelson, E. C. (1997) Patrick Browne's *The Civil and Natural History of Jamaica* (1756, 1789). *Archives of Natural History*. 24 (3). 326–36.

Nunberg, G. (1993) The Places of Books in the Age of Electronic Reproduction. *Representations*. (42), 13–37.

Overholt, J. (2015) Together, We Can FrEEBO. *Medium*, https://medium.com/@john_overholt/together-we-can-freebo-b33d39618f8 (Accessed 20 January 2020).

Pauley, B. (2009) Eighteenth-Century Book Tracker. *Early Modern Online Bibliography*, https://earlymodernonlinebib.wordpress.com/2009/08/12/eighteenth-century-book-tracker/ (Accessed 21 January 2020).

Pearson, D. (2008) *Books As History: The Importance of Books beyond Their Texts*. London: British Library.

Power, E. B. (1990) *Edition of One: The Autobiography of Eugene B. Power Founder of University Microfilms*. Ann Arbor: University Microfilms Incorporated.

Prescott, A. (2016) What Price Gale Cengage? *Digital Riffs*, https://medium.com/digital-riffs/what-price-gale-cengage-668d358ce5cd (Accessed 10 July 2018).

Prescott, A. (2018) Searching for Dr Johnson: The Digitization of the Burney Newspaper Collection. In S. G. Brandtzæg, P. Goring, & C. Watson (eds.) *Travelling Chronicles: News and Newspapers from the Early Modern Period to the Eighteenth Century*. Brill: Leiden. pp. 49–71.

Quint, B. (2002) Gale Group to Digitize Most 18th-Century English-Language Books, Doubles InfoTrac Holdings. *Newsbreaks*, http://news breaks.infotoday.com/NewsBreaks/Gale-Group-to-Digitize-Most-18thCentury-EnglishLanguage-Books-Doubles-InfoTrac-Holdings-17156.asp (Accessed 5 September 2019).

Rand, J. & Fust, K. (2019) Gale Primary Sources and Gale Literature Product Enhancements Launching in December 2019, https://blog.gale.com/gale-primary-sources-and-gale-literature-product-enhancements-launching-in-december-2019/ (Accessed 11 November 2019).

Rather, L. J. & Wiggins, B. (1989) Henriette D. Avram. *American Libraries*. October. 855–9.

Reill, P. (2009) A Message from ASECS President Peter Reill. *Early Modern Online Bibliography*, https://earlymodernonlinebib.wordpress.com/2009/12/03/a-message-from-asecs-president-peter-reill/ (Accessed 24 January 2020).

Research Publications (1987) Microfilm Selection Criteria. Letter to Subscribing Libraries.

Research Publications (1994) The Eighteenth Century. Brochure.

Risam, R. (2015) Beyond the Margins: Intersectionality and the Digital Humanities. *Digital Humanities Quarterly*. 9 (2), http://digitalhuma nities.org:8081/dhq/vol/9/2/000208/000208.html (Accessed 21 July 2020).

Risam, R. (2018) *New Digital Worlds: Postcolonial Digital Humanities in Theory, Praxis, and Pedagogy*. Evanston, IL: Northwestern University Press.

Robinson, P. (1993) *The Digitization of Primary Textual Sources*. London: Office for Humanities Communication.

Rogers, M. (2007) Gale/ProQuest Titles Linking. *Library Journal*. 132 (20). 32–32.

Saffedy, W. (2000) *Micrographics: Technology for the 21st Century*. Prairie Village, KS: ARMA International.

Schonfeld, R. C. (2003) *JSTOR: A History*. Princeton, NJ: Princeton University Press.

Schwarz, L. (2004) Eighteenth Century Collections Online (A Thomson Gale Digital Archive). *Reviews in History*. (408). https://reviews.his tory.ac.uk/review/408 (Accessed 27 July 2020).

Sherratt, T. (2013) From Portals to Platforms: Building New Frameworks for User Engagement. Presented at the LIANZA 2013 Conference 2013. Hamilton, New Zealand, www.nla.gov.au/our-publications/staff-papers/from-portal-to-platform# (Accessed 19 March 2020).

Sherratt, T. (2019) Hacking Heritage: Understanding the Limits of Online Access. In H. Lewi, W. Smith, D. vom Lehn, & S. Cooke (eds.) *The Routledge International Handbook of New Digital Practices in Galleries, Libraries, Archives, Museums and Heritage Sites*. London: Routledge. Author Accepted Manuscript version, https://timsherratt.org/blog/hacking-heritage/ (Accessed 8 August 2020)

Shevlin, E. (2009) Unequal Access and Commercial Databases. *Early Modern Online Bibliography*, https://earlymodernonlinebib.wordpress .com/2009/12/09/unequal-access-and-commercial-databases/ (Accessed 5 November 2019).

Shevlin, E. (2010) Gale's ECCO and BiblioLife: Print-on-Demand Initiatives. *Early Modern Online Bibliography*, https://earlymodernonli nebib.wordpress.com/2010/08/12/gales-ecco-and-bibliolife-print-on-demand-initiatives/ (Accessed 21 April 2020).

Smith, D. & Cordell, R. (2018) A Research Agenda for Historical and Multilingual Optical Character Recognition: Historical and Multilingual OCR, https://ocr.northeastern.edu/report/ (Accessed 30 January 2020).

Smith, J. (2003) Gale, ProQuest Hope to Find New Money in Old Documents. *Crain's Detroit Business*, www.crainsdetroit.com/article/20030818/SUB/308180861/gale-proquest-hope-to-find-new-money-in-old-documents (Accessed 27 February 2019).

Snyder, H. (2003) The Future of the ESTC: A Vision. In H. Snyder & M. S. Smith (eds.) *The English Short Title Catalogue: Past, Present, Future*. New York: AMS Press. pp. 21–30.

Snyder, H. & Smith, M. S. (eds.) (2003) *The English Short Title Catalogue: Past, Present, Future*. New York: AMS Press.

Somers, J. (2017) Torching the Modern-Day Library of Alexandria. *The Atlantic*, www.theatlantic.com/technology/archive/2017/04/the-tragedy-of-google-books/523320/?utm_source=atltw (Accessed 21 October 2020).

Spedding, P. (2011) 'The New Machine': Discovering the Limits of ECCO. *Eighteenth-Century Studies*. 44 (4). 437–53.

Tanner, S., Muñoz, T. , & Ros, P. H. (2009) Measuring Mass Text Digitization Quality and Usefulness: Lessons Learned from Assessing the OCR Accuracy of the British Library's 19th Century Online Newspaper Archive. *D-Lib Magazine*. 15 (7/8), www.dlib.org/dlib/july09/munoz/07munoz.html (Accessed 18 December 2019).

Tanselle, G. T. (2001) Not the Real Thing. *The Times Literary Supplement*. 24 14 August.

Thompson, J. B. (2005) *Books in the Digital Age*. Cambridge: Polity.

Thylstrup, N. B. (2018) *The Politics of Mass Digitization*. Cambridge, MA: MIT Press.

Tolonen, M. S., Mäkelä, E. , Ijaz, A. , & and Lahti, L. (forthcoming 2021). Corpus Linguistics and Eighteenth Century Collections Online (ECCO). *Research in Corpus Linguistics*.

Trettien, W. A. (2013) A Deep History of Electronic Textuality: The Case of *English Reprints of Jhon Milton's Areopagitica*. *Digital Humanities*

Quarterly. 7 (1), www.digitalhumanities.org/dhq/vol/7/1/000150/000150.html (Accessed 8 May 2020).

Trouillot, M.-R. (2015) *Silencing the Past (20th Anniversary Edition): Power and the Production of History*. Boston, MA: Beacon Press.

Warnock, J. (1991) The Camelot Project, https://web.archive.org/web/20090304134754/ http://www.planetpdf.com/planetpdf/pdfs/warnock_camelot.pdf (Accessed 20 July 2020).

Weinberger, D. (2012) Library As Platform. *Library Journal*, www.libraryjournal.com?detailStory=by-david-weinberger (Accessed 19 March 2020).

Wells, H. G. (1938) *World Brain*. Garden City, N.Y., Doubleday, Doran & Company. Internet Archive: http://archive.org/details/worldbrain00wells (Accessed 22 October 2019).

Werner, S. (2012) Where Material Book Culture Meets Digital Humanities. *Journal of Digital Humanities*. 1 (3), http://journalofdigitalhumanities .org/1–3/where-material-book-culture-meets-digital-humanities-by-sarah-werner/ (Accessed 15 April 2020).

Werner, S. (2019) *Studying Early Printed Books 1450–1800*. Chichester: Wiley Blackwell.

Wexler, E. (2015) Subscription Scare Fuels Worries over Who Controls Data That Scholars Need. *The Chronicle of Higher Education*. 15 October, www.chronicle.com/article/Subscription-Scare-Fuels/234003 (Accessed 22 June 2018).

Wikipedia Contributors (2019) BiblioBazaar. *Wikipedia*, https://en.wikipedia.org/w/index.php?title=BiblioBazaar&oldid=884491573 (Accessed 25 July 2019).

Wisbey, R. (1962) Concordance Making by Electronic Computer: Some Experiences with the 'Wiener Genesis'. *The Modern Language Review*. 57 (2). 161–72.

Zeeman, J. C. (1980) On Bibliographical Standards. *Factotum: Newsletter of the XVIIIth Century STC* (no. 8). April. 2–4.

Personal Communications

Bankoski, R. (2019a) Email to Stephen Gregg, 16 July.

Bankoski, R. (2019b) Email to Stephen Gregg, 28 May.

Bankoski, R. (2020) Email to Megan Sullivan, forwarded to Stephen Gregg, 30 June.

Bankoski, R. & De Mowbray, J. (2019) Video conference call with Stephen Gregg, 14 August.

Blaney, J. (2019) Email to Stephen Gregg, 2 December.

Cook, K. S. (2019) Email to Stephen Gregg, 4 July.

De Mowbray, J. (2019a) Email to Stephen Gregg, 16 July.

De Mowbray, J. (2019b) Email to Stephen Gregg, 16 September.

De Mowbray, J. (2019c) Email to Stephen Gregg, 28 May.

De Mowbray, J. (2020a) Email to Stephen Gregg, 22 January.

De Mowbray, J. (2020b) Email to Stephen Gregg, 20 July.

Geiger, B. K. & Schilling, V. (2016) Email to Scott Gibbens, forwarded to Stephen Gregg, 26 April.

Gibbens, S. (2019) Email to Stephen Gregg, 25 October.

Houghton, C. (2019) Email to Stephen Gregg, 31 July.

Houghton, C. (2020) Email to Stephen Gregg, 13 January.

Kumar, N. (2019) Email to Julia de Mowbray, forwarded to Stephen Gregg, 1 November.

Mandell, L. (2019a) Video conference call with Stephen Gregg, 27 November.

Mandell, L. (2019b) Email to Stephen Gregg, 20 December.

Marchionni, P. & Milloy, C. (2020) Video conference call with Stephen Gregg, 3 March.

Schaffner, P. (2019). Email to Stephen Gregg, 19 November.

Sullivan, M. (2020) Email to Stephen Gregg, 16 January.

Illustrations

Images of *The Civil and Natural History of Jamaica* (1756), *The Works of Alexander Pope* (1736), *A Narrative of the Life of Mrs Charlotte Charke* (1755, and second edition), Laurence Sterne, *The Life and Opinions of Tristram*

Shandy (1775), and of the microfilm reader are reproduced here with permission from the British Library. Images of *The Civil and Natural History of Jamaica* (1789) are reproduced courtesy of Kansas University Libraries. The image of the hand-press is reproduced by kind permission of the St. Bride Foundation.

Acknowledgements

I'd like to thank the people at Gale-Cengage who have shared bits of history, documents, files, and some explanations: Ray Bankoski, Seth Cayley, Julia de Mowbray, Chris Houghton, Megan Sullivan, and Margaret Walligora. I'd also like to acknowledge the wonderfully helpful conversations I've had with Jonathan Blaney; Stephen Brooks, Paola Marchionni, and Caren Milloy at Jisc; Brian Geiger at the ESTC; Scott Gibbens; Elspeth Healey and Karen Severud Cook at the Kenneth Spencer Library; Natraj Kumar of HTC Global; Laura Mandell; Andrew Prescott; Paul Schaffner of the TCP; and Mikko Tolonen. My thanks too for the helpful comments of my reviewers and my editor, Jane Winters. My reading of old books would have been a poor affair without the indefatigable guidance from my colleague, Ian Gadd. Finally, a big thank you to my wife, Nicky, and my family.

Cambridge Elements ≡

Publishing and Book Culture

SERIES EDITOR
Samantha Rayner
University College London

Samantha Rayner is a Reader in UCL's Department of
Information Studies. She is also Director of UCL's Centre for
Publishing, co-Director of the Bloomsbury CHAPTER
(Communication History, Authorship, Publishing, Textual
Editing and Reading) and co-editor of the Academic Book of
the Future BOOC (Book as Open Online Content) with UCL
Press.

ASSOCIATE EDITOR
Leah Tether
University of Bristol

Leah Tether is Professor of Medieval Literature and Publishing
at the University of Bristol. With an academic background in
medieval French and English literature and a professional
background in trade publishing, Leah has combined her
expertise and developed an international research profile in
book and publishing history from manuscript to digital.

ADVISORY BOARD

Simone Murray, Monash University

Claire Squires, University of Stirling

Andrew Nash, University of London

Leslie Howsam, Ryerson University

David Finkelstein, University of Edinburgh

Alexis Weedon, University of Bedfordshire

Alan Staton, Booksellers Association

Angus Phillips, Oxford International Centre for Publishing

Richard Fisher, Yale University Press

John Maxwell, Simon Fraser University

Shafquat Towheed, The Open University

Jen McCall, Emerald Publishing

About the Series

This series aims to fill the demand for easily accessible, quality texts available for teaching and research in the diverse and dynamic fields of Publishing and Book Culture. Rigorously researched and peer-reviewed Elements will be published under themes, or 'Gatherings'. These Elements should be the first check point for researchers or students working on that area of publishing and book trade history and practice: we hope that, situated so logically at Cambridge University Press, where academic publishing in the UK began, it will develop to create an unrivalled space where these histories and practices can be investigated and preserved.

Cambridge Elements ⯐

Publishing and Book Culture

ACADEMIC PUBLISHING
Gathering Editor: Jane Winters

Jane Winters is Professor of Digital Humanities at the School of Advanced Study, University of London. She is co-convenor of the Royal Historical Society's open-access monographs series, New Historical Perspectives, and a member of the International Editorial Board of Internet Histories and the Academic Advisory Board of the Open Library of Humanities.

ELEMENTS IN THE GATHERING

The General Reader and the Academy: Medieval French Literature and Penguin Classics
Leah Tether

The Edited Collection: Pasts, Present and Futures
Peter Webster

Reading Peer Review
Martin Paul Eve, Cameron Neylon, Daniel Paul O'Donnell, Samuel Moore, Robert Gadie, Victoria Odeniyi and Shahina Parvin

A full series listing is available at: www.cambrige.org/EPBC